Classic
PASTA
C·U·I·S·I·N·E

Edited by Rosemary Moon

SMITHMARK

ILLUSTRATIONS BY
CAMILLA SOPWITH, ROD FREELING AND LAWRIE TAYLOR

CLB 4362
© 1995 CLB Publishing

This edition published in 1995 by Smithmark Publishers, Inc.
16 East 32nd Street, New York NY 10016

SMITHMARK books are available for bulk purchase for sales promotion
and premium use. For details write or call the manager of special sales,
SMITHMARK Publishers, Inc.
16 East 32nd Street, New York,
NY 10016; (212) 532-6600

Produced by CLB Publishing
Godalming Business Centre
Woolsack Way, Godalming, Surrey, UK

ISBN 0-8317-1123-X

Printed in South Africa
10 9 8 7 6 5 4 3 2 1

CONTENTS

INTRODUCTION

Pasta must be one of the most popular and versatile foods in the world! It has been a staple part of the diet in Italy and China for centuries and, although many other nations have only recently accepted it as part of their regular eating pattern, records show that in many countries pasta consumption is increasing at a rate of around twenty percent per person per year.

What is Pasta?

Pasta is a very simple, natural food. When made at home, it is a dough of flour and eggs, with perhaps a little olive oil added for extra flavor. The commercial dried pasta is made from the finest of all hard wheats, durum wheat, which is ground and then made into a dough with just water. Some commercial pastas are enriched with egg, but, in most cases, dried pasta contains only minimal amounts of fat, making it an ideal food for those following a low-fat or weight-reducing diet. (Of course served in the traditional Italian way, with plenty of butter and olive oil, the benefits of it as a diet food become a little less obvious!)

Pasta is a generic name that covers a vast number of shapes of dough, and fresh and dried varieties in many different colors. I have read that there are around six hundred different commercial pastas, but the selection available at the average supermarket is more than enough to provide plenty of variety for even the most regular of pasta-eaters, and will certainly be sufficient for you when preparing the recipes in this book.

Chinese or Italian

I am not brave enough to voice an opinion as to who first came up with the idea of making and eating pasta. Of course the Italians would tell you that it is their invention, their national food and that should anyone try to say that it is not an Italian creation, then they are quite definitely out of order. It must be borne in mind, however, that when Marco Polo journeyed from Italy to China in 1270, he reported in detail on the Chinese habit of eating noodles, and many people have supposed that he then brought pasta back to Italy with him. Vermicelli or noodles were nevertheless an established part of the Italian diet well before the thirteenth century, which raises more than a little doubt about the story of the traveling Italian and his booty. It is said that noodles have been eaten in China for around 6000 years, but then records in the Spaghetti Museum in Pontedassio on the Italian Riviera claim that pasta has been a staple part of the Italian diet since 5000 B.C. It is said that the ancient Etruscans ate flat strips from a dough cake called *laganon*, a word of remarkable similarity to the modern word for flat strips of pasta dough – lasagne.

Pasta Doesn't Grow on Trees

I shall remain neutral in the argument about the origins of pasta, safely sitting on the fence! It must be true that for as long as man has grown wheat and has had the ability to grind it, and then to mix the resulting flour with eggs or water, he has had the potential to make pasta. Whoever made it first is irrelevant – unless you are Chinese or Italian and passionate about pasta!

One thing, however, is certain. Pasta does not grow on trees! It is now several decades since the distinguished commentator, Richard Dimbleby confused UK television viewers with a more than plausible April Fool, showing the spaghetti harvest with many Italian workers plucking the pasta, ripened in the sun, from the branches of laden trees. The spaghetti harvest was a marvelous piece of broadcasting fun which has been remembered for years.

An Italian Way of Life

I know that I am going to write far more about pasta in connection with the Italians than the Chinese, but that should not be interpreted as meaning that I am attributing the origins of pasta to the Italians and not to their rivals! It is simply that, for most of us, Italy appears to be the home of pasta because the Italians eat so much of it and many of the classic pasta recipes originate from there.

I have become convinced in my own mind that the Mediterranean sun has a great influence on people's attitude toward food. It seems that the long, hot days dictate a slower pace of life, allowing more time for people to prepare their food at home using fresh ingredients. There is no doubt at all that the pleasure associated with eating freshly cooked, homemade pasta is immeasurable against that of eating even the very best of dried pastas, so it has been traditional for centuries for the Italians to prepare their pasta at home.

Pasta is traditionally mixed and kneaded by hand, and then rolled out to a paper-like thinness on a tabletop, using an exceptionally long rolling pin made specifically for the task. The dough becomes difficult to manage for the uninitiated, but those with years of practise have a method to insure perfect results every time. Space is the main consideration, as a large area is required to be able to roll the dough thinly without having to stop and reshape it.

The easiest pasta shapes to prepare by hand are lasagne, tagliatelle and a flat spaghetti. For many of us, the art of intricate pasta-shaping is something yet to be mastered!

The Advent of the Pasta Machine

I am not a great one for gadgets in the kitchen, preferring a set of sharp knives to a cabinet full of electrical wizardry that seldom gets used. I am, however, dedicated to my pasta machine to the extent that I have even clamped it to my kitchen work-table in a very prominent position. In the modern kitchen one thing that is not available is space, and there simply isn't enough work surface to roll dough by hand until it is thin enough to make good, light pasta. A pasta machine which passes the dough through a series of rollers until it is ready to be shaped and cooked saves so much time and space, is, I believe, indispensable for modern cooks who wish to make their own pasta regularly in a typical modern kitchen.

I have been intrigued to read of the attitude of some of our leading chefs to pasta-making in the plethora of cookbooks which now reveal the secrets of their restaurant successes. In one of my favorite books, *Leaves from the Walnut Tree* by Ann and Franco Taruschio, Franco describes how he always used to make pasta by hand but, having used standard rolling machines, he now uses an electric pasta-maker which can produce almost any shape. However, he is adamant that no machine can make pasta quite as perfectly as that which is made by hand. It may then be argued that the pasta machine has caused a drop in the quality of homemade pasta. That may be so for those endowed with long rolling pins and large work surfaces, but for most of us it has opened up a whole new perspective on one of the greatest of culinary pleasures – homemade pasta cookery.

The Ancient Pasta Wars

One of the reasons why there are so many pasta shapes is because of fierce and intense competition between the main pasta-makers during the Italian Renaissance in the fifteenth and sixteenth centuries. They were always wanting a new shape, something different for their representatives to show, to secure an extra segment in what was a highly competitive market, even by modern standards. Of course there is no need for so

11

many shapes and I am certain that only the largest of supermarkets or a specialty Italian store would ever stock more than about twenty varieties of pasta today. Pasta takes up so much room on a shelf, and it would be impossible to display more than a fairly limited number of packages. I know that when I had a deli, the maximum number of shapes which I ever stocked was ten.

The competition between pasta manufacturers is still intense, both in Italy and abroad. It is difficult to find a new sales story for a product that is basically so simple and natural. What is more interesting to me is the way in which such rivalry is now being extended to a whole new ancillary industry, that of prepared pasta sauces. Certainly in the UK this is one of the fastest growing sectors of the food market and competition is very hot. However, as pasta is such a natural product, I think it is important to insure that the sauce or sauce base that you purchase, if indeed you do so, is as natural as possible with no additives. When I buy such products, I always ignore the leading brand names and go for the all-natural sauces clearly labeled as additive-free, or an Italian produced sauce base, again with no additives.

Fresh or Dried

You might well expect me to say here that fresh pasta is always better than dried, and that the latter should only be resorted to in moments of utter desperation, or when the last egg in your kitchen has been used and all the stores are shut. Well, that's not the case at all!

I have to say that I do think homemade pasta is always better than bought, and that it is immeasurably superior to commercially prepared fresh pasta. I always find the fresh pasta available in supermarkets too thick, and consequently heavy to eat. Fresh pasta in sealed packages will keep for about 4-5 days, and many people do like to keep a packet or two in the freezer for emergency use. However, I always choose to use a dried pasta if I don't have time to make my own, as I actually prefer the texture of the dried product.

Having stated my reservations, there is no doubt that fresh pasta is becoming a very popular item in most large supermarkets, where more and more colors and shapes are being introduced. One supermarket near my home sells fresh tomato and black pastas, the latter being colored with squid ink. I have noticed that the thinner shapes such as spaghetti are the most popular.

There's Dried and Dried

There are basically two types of pastas – *pasta all'uovo* or *pasta fatta in casa*, that is homemade egg pasta, or *pasta secca*, the commercial dried pasta made from a flour and water paste. You may well consider that all dried pastas must be the same, but there is a world of difference in quality between them, and you definitely get what you pay for when it comes to pasta. Most supermarkets sell their own brand, and there are plenty of proprietary products which are very well known. All are adequate, but they simply do not compare to the Italian dried pastas which are available in delis, specialty food stores and even in some of the flagship branches of the major supermarket chains. The Italian pasta has a much firmer texture, and is more akin to a homemade pasta when cooked.

I recently met up with a cousin whom I had not seen for some time at a wedding. She said that she had read an article that I had written expressing the same views on the merits of Italian dried pasta as I have just expounded. Since then, Andrea has bought nothing except the Italian product, and has been delighted with the quality and the improved flavor and texture. (I always feel that I am winning when the family start to take notice!)

A Limited Selection

The only drawback to making your own pasta is that you are somewhat limited in the number of shapes that you can produce. They are mostly flat, folded or rolled, as they have to come from a flat sheet of dough. I make more tagliatelli at home than anything else – it is easy as it is one of the three "shapes" on the pasta machine. The basic dough is rolled into strips or lasagne, and then there are two extra sets of cutters on the standard machine for tagliatelli and flat spaghetti. The lasagne may be cut and made into ravioli or cannelloni, but there is certainly no way of making macaroni or pasta shells. However, small rectangles of pasta may be pinched together in the centre, having been cut with a wheel cutter, to form farfalle, pasta butterflies or bows.

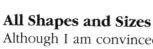

All Shapes and Sizes

Although I am convinced that some of the six hundred names attributed to pasta shapes must be duplicates, there is no doubt at all that there are literally hundreds of different varieties of pasta. I know that there are some duplicates because there is one very famous example. The town of Bologna in the Emilia-Romagna region is *the* gastronomic centre of northern Italy. It has many claims to fame in the culinary world, and is the very heart of the Lambrusco grape-growing region. It is renowned for its meat sauces and also for one specific type of pasta, tagliatelle. Like spaghetti, this is an ideal shape for mixing with a smooth sauce, becoming evenly coated with the delicious juices and granules of ingredients. However, just down the expressway in the Italian capital, tagliatelle, the beloved specialty of Bologna, is widely referred to as fettuccini, a favorite pasta of the Romans. I suppose it's a bit like the confusion between the English and Scots over rutabagas and turnips!

Different Shapes for Different Dishes

I always divide pastas into five main groups, according to how they are to be cooked and served:

Pastas for coating with a smooth sauce are the most popular group. These include spaghetti, tagliatelle and all the various thicknesses of vermicelli. When eating Italian, do as the Italians do! They would never sit down to a mound of spaghetti with a dollop of Bolognese sauce atop the mountain! Even if the dish is brought to the table in such a way, the sauce is tossed into the pasta before serving, coating the strands evenly to produce a dish of wonderful flavors. Try it – it's so much better than the mountaineering approach!

Surprise Pastas is my name for the shapes which can harbor the good bits of a sauce! I include shells, penne, large macaroni and farfalle, and the countless other shapes that have recesses to catch shrimp, pine nuts, diced vegetables and globules of dressing, giving surprise mouthfuls of tangy flavor in the middle of a dish.

Pastas for stuffing should contain their filling during the cooking process. The two most popular varieties are ravioli and cannelloni. Stuffed ravioli are available ready prepared, the fresh varieties being a great improvement over the canned in tomato sauce, which is a travesty of good Italian cooking. However, making ravioli at home allows for far more creative fillings. Cannelloni should be crisp on top, either from broiling or from baking in a very hot oven, while remaining tender and moist underneath.

Pastas for baking are usually boiled before being included in a composite dish to be baked in the oven, or *al forno*. The most obvious is lasagne, the broad sheets of pasta so easily produced by a domestic pasta machine. However, large macaroni and penne may also be baked, and are both especially attractive when lined up neatly to form a layer in a dish that is to be cut when served.

Small pastas for soup are known collectively as pastini. They are tiny so that they will cook quickly and blend in well with other ingredients in the soup, yet remain easy to eat with a spoon. Pastini are also useful for sweet pasta dishes.

The most popular of the pasta shapes are:

Spaghetti, long fine strands of pasta, is, without doubt, the most popular shape in the world. It is available in different thicknesses, and I like to use a fine spaghetti, the finest of which is called spaghettini. Italian spaghetti has the best texture.

Vermicelli is one of the Italian names for the pasta that would be referred to as fine noodles in China. Another Italian name is capellini and the very finest variety is called *capelli d'angelo*, or angel's hair. Vermicelli are used in soups or broken up in sweet dishes, and may also be used to create pasta nests, which are deep-fried and then used as baskets for serving designer savory dishes.

Tagliatelle is probably my favorite pasta. It is thin ribbons of dough that should be only about ¼ inch thick, and it is an excellent vehicle for any number of sauces. I think it is easier to eat than spaghetti as, being flat, it cannot slide off a fork so easily!

Lasagne are the broad sheets of pasta most frequently used for baking in a dish of meat, fish or vegetable sauce, which is then usually topped with a white sauce and grated cheese. Homemade lasagne is always flat, but dried lasagne can be bought with a decorative ruffled edge. Lasagne should be boiled before it is baked, and this is best done a few sheets at a time – any more and the pasta will stick together in the pan. Easy-cook lasagne is available which requires no pre-cooking, but it bears a remarkable resemblance to cardboard when compared to the fresh pasta.

Cannelloni tubes are easily made at home from a basic lasagne, then par-boiled and dried over a broom handle before stuffing (that is, a broom handle kept specifically for pasta-making duties, and not used at other times for beating carpets, etc!). If buying dried cannelloni shells, check the package carefully before purchasing to insure that there are no broken tubes underneath the top layer of pasta. A broken cannelloni shell is of little use to anyone.

Ravioli are little packages of pasta, usually with a savory filling. Ravioli pans are available, whereby a sheet of pasta is laid over the pan and filling is added where the recesses are marked. A second sheet of pasta is then laid over the first, and a rolling pin is passed over the top. This forces the filling down into the recesses of the ravioli molds, and seals the pasta sheets together around the filling while cutting the dough into squares over the perforations of the pan. This produces small ravioli which are ideal for cooking in a soup. Ravioli are always served in a sauce.

Tortellini are small, filled pastas which may be homemade, although the folding requires some skill to keep the filling enclosed. They are available dried and are ideal emergency food, for the occasion when you really do not want to cook. Tortellini should be served in a sauce; otherwise they are dry. Legend says that the shape of this pasta is modeled on Venus's navel – I wonder how she would have responded to the fact that some people now refer to tortellini as pasta dumplings?

Pastini is the collective name for tiny pasta shapes suitable for cooking in soup, or *in brodo*. Some of the most inventive shapes are within this group – there are alphabet letters, space invaders, tiny flowers and all sorts of cartoon characters. Many shapes of pastini are sold ready-cooked in a sauce as children's food for serving on toast, but this is definitely not a traditional presentation.

Fusilli are pasta spirals and, marvelous for catching little globules of sauce within their coils. Their attractive shapes also make them an ideal pasta for serving cold in salads. Fusilli was one of the first shapes to be available as tri-colored pasta, dried from the supermarket shelf. The colors are usually yellow (eggs), green (spinach) and red (tomato).

Farfalle are another decorative shape, this time resembling bows. Sauce collects in the middle, in the ruches, so this is another pasta to serve with tasty, savory sauces. I think that farfalle make a particularly attractive appetizer.

Conchiglie or shells are made in various sizes, from pastini right up to large shells which may be stuffed and served as an appetizer. The medium-sized ones are popular as they too trap mouthfuls of delicious sauce to create surprise bursts of flavor.

Macaroni is available in two types – straight and elbow, the latter having a slight kink in the middle. It is said that the Holy Roman Emperor Frederick II was so fond of this shape that he named it macaroni after *marcus* – the divine dish. Macaroni comes in various thicknesses, but it always has a hole through the middle. I used to sell long macaroni, the length of spaghetti, when I had my deli, and it was very popular. It can be used to line a pudding basin, resembling an old-fashioned beehive, which can then be filled and baked or steamed. However, I have not seen long macaroni now for several years, and that which is generally available is referred to as short-cut.

Penne is another of my favorite pastas, being tubes cut on the slant of about ½-inch diameter when dry, and which trap mouthfuls of flavor when mixed with a sauce. Penne are available plain or lightly ribbed – I prefer the latter.

Rigatoni is another tube variety of pasta, this time straight cut and almost always ribbed. The name is derived from the Italian word *riga*, which means line.

Cappelletti are one of the few shapes that can be made easily at home. They are more attractive with a fluted edge, so cut them out of a strip of dough using a fluted canapé cutter. To achieve the cap shape, press the dough into the palm of one hand with the opposite thumb, turning the thumb gently to form the indentation.

Ruoti are pasta wheels, and are available in various sizes. They are an attractive shape to use in soups or cold, in pasta salads.

Gnocchi, like conchiglie, also resemble small shells, and are an excellent shape for salads and hot dishes where there are tasty morsels to be trapped within the pasta.

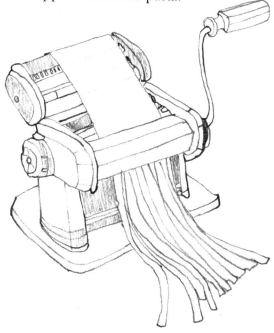

Pasta Extrusion

Many of the shapes described here are extruded through a machine which forces the dough into shape under a certain amount of pressure. There are domestic versions of pasta extruders, one of which is an attachment for a table food mixer. These, however, tend to be slow and labored in their task and may take almost half an hour to extrude sufficient pasta to feed four or six people, the dough for which must be of just the right consistency. On balance, and I have owned both types of machine, I prefer the pasta roller, despite its more limited potential for producing shapes.

The Basic Pasta Dough

Pasta dough is simply a mixture of flour and eggs, with a little water or olive oil if necessary for flavor, or to bind the dough together. My basic recipe for four to six people is:

4 cups white bread flour
4 eggs, lightly beaten
Olive oil or water, if necessary

Put the flour into a large mixing bowl, and make a well in the center. Add the beaten eggs, and bring the mixture together, using first a fork and then your fingers. Add a few drops of oil or water if the dough is too dry. Gather the dough up into a ball, then knead it with the heel of your hand until it is smooth, shiny and no longer sticky. Cover the dough in plastic wrap, and leave it in a cool place to rest for 30 minutes if you are to roll it by hand. If you are going to be using a pasta machine, you can press on with the rolling and shaping of the pasta straightaway. Allowing the dough to rest helps to prevent it from springing back out of shape during rolling by hand.

I generally use AA large eggs when making pasta, and find that just the four eggs are sufficient to make the dough without any extra oil. However, all flours vary in the amount of liquid that they will absorb, so it is as well to be prepared to add a little extra moisture if required.

A Drier Dough Gives Better Results

The easiest mistake to make when producing homemade pasta is to make the dough too wet. Although it will feel good to handle it will not cut readily in a pasta machine, and the strands will have more of a tendency to stick together during cooking. The dough should be dry but not quite crumbly. You should not require much additional flour on the work surface to prevent the dough from sticking, and you may find that you have to pass it through the rollers of a pasta machine twice on setting one to achieve a smooth sheet of pasta without splits. However, after the initial rolling, the dough will be easy to handle, and will fall readily into strands if cut by machine into tagliatelle or spaghetti.

Salt in the Dough or Salt in the Water?

Many pasta recipes call for a good pinch of salt to be added to the flour before the dough is mixed. I am of the school of thought that says this has a tendency to make the dough tough, and that it is better to add the salt to the water when cooking the pasta. This is especially true when making whole wheat pasta.

Fine Flour for Whole Wheat Varieties

I always think that commercial whole wheat pasta is wooden in texture and totally lacking in flavor. However, homemade whole wheat pasta is delicious and totally unlike the commercial alternative. To make a good dough it is essential that you use a fine whole wheat flour – bread flour is not suitable as it has too much bran in too large flakes which will cause the dough to tear. I use the same quantities of flour and eggs as for the basic egg dough, but always add one tablespoon of olive oil with the eggs. This helps to start the binding of the dough, and more can be added if necessary. Whole wheat pasta tends to be a little drier than the egg variety, so the dough should be carefully monitored during mixing.

Musical Pasta?

Pasta verde is not an opera, it is a green dough colored and flavored with spinach! The quantities of flour and eggs are slightly different to those for the standard doughs as some spinach purée has to be incorporated into the mixture with the eggs. A good basic recipe is:

2½ cups white bread flour
2 eggs, lightly beaten
⅔ cup finely chopped or puréed, cooked spinach
Olive oil, if necessary

Sift the flour into a mixing bowl, and make a well in the center. Beat together the eggs and the spinach purée, and add them to the flour. Mix with a fork and then with your hands until the dough can be gathered into a ball. Add a little oil if the mixture is too dry, and a little flour if it is too wet. Knead lightly, until the dough is smooth and shiny and the spinach has evenly colored it. Cover and rest for 30 minutes before rolling by hand or machine.

The Technicolor Cook

Once you start making pasta you will want to experiment with all sorts of colorings and flavors. Finely chopped herbs produce an attractive green fleck in yellow egg pasta, whilst a dramatic yellow color may be produced by adding a few teaspoons of saffron or turmeric infusion – the former has the more subtle flavor. Beet and tomato purées both produce red doughs, while carrot gives a good orange color. Perhaps the most dramatic of all is black pasta which is colored with squid ink. It has little flavor but looks stunning when served with seafood in a cream sauce.

Rules for Cooking Perfect Pasta

There are a few basic guidelines to follow to produce perfect pasta, which apply to both dried and fresh varieties. They are:

* Always cook pasta in a large pan in plenty of boiling salted water. This will help to prevent it from sticking together during cooking.

* Do not overcook pasta. It should be tender but still firm, with a little bite. This is called *al dente*. Fresh pasta will take only a minute or so to cook, and is ready when it floats to the top of the pan.

* Rinse pasta in boiling or cold water after cooking, depending on how it is to be used. This helps to wash away any surplus starch.

* Do not drain cooked pasta too vigorously: give the colander a brief, firm shake, then leave it to drain. Shake too much and the pasta will stick together.

* When boiling lasagne, only add a few sheets at a time to the pan, then lay the par-boiled sheets on clean dishcloths until required.

Fun for All the Family

Pasta-making is great fun and even the youngest child who wants to help in the kitchen can enjoy turning the handle of the pasta machine. I talk to more and more people who tell me that pasta-making is now a family activity with everyone involved, and enjoying it. It is not complicated and is a beginning for would-be-cooks in the kitchen, having far more relevance to our modern way of life than the little cakes that I started baking as a child.

After teaching at a cookery vacation course for 10-14 year olds, I was interested to read the questionnaires that were filled in by the participants at the end of the week. The children were of very mixed culinary ability when they arrived and one little girl of ten, who had done next-to-no cooking before the vacation, commented that making pasta for the first evening's dinner had been her favorite thing as she had never cooked a real meal before – an excellent way to start!

Oriental Pastas

Although Chinese egg noodles are very similar to the Italian egg pasta, there are other oriental pastas that are very different indeed. These include rice noodles which are long spaghetti-like strands. They are seldom cut, and are sold folded back on themselves in very long lengths. Some rice noodles are as thin as vermicelli, and these are most often used as a thickening for clear Chinese soups. The Chinese developed rice noodles because wheat is only grown in the north of the country, and rice is the staple food in all other areas.

Cellophane noodles are not an oriental attempt at recycling unwanted packaging! They are actually made from a paste of ground mung beans and are virtually transparent, which has led to their unusual name. Cellophane noodles are very fine, and are soaked before being added to stir-fries; they do not require boiling before they are used.

The last of the oriental noodles in common use is Japanese menrui. Menrui is actually a general name for noodles made from either wheat or buckwheat. They are sold in varying thicknesses, and are usually boiled. Menrui are, however, cooked to a much softer texture than the *al dente* of the regular egg noodles.

All pasta is fun to cook. Try making your own dough, and discover the true delights of this simple and versatile food.

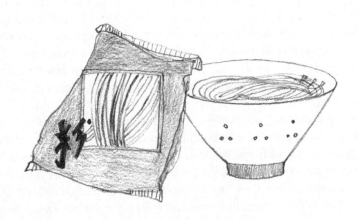

SOUPS

For many centuries most meals were soups in one form or another. This was for the simple reason that the only real cooking facility available in any home, even those of the wealthy, was an iron pot hanging over an open fire. These soups were the original one-pot meals. In the households of the wealthy the meal would have been more akin to a stew with plenty of meat and vegetables, but in the poorer homes, where the resources and ingredients were much less, the meal became watered down into a soup. Different vegetables, cereals or grains were used to thicken the soups and give more substance to the meal, according to the cuisine of the area. Root vegetables and eventually potatoes were popular thickening agents in many countries, as well as grains such as pearl barley, rice or lentils. In China and Italy, however, it was pasta or noodles that were used to thicken the soups and to add body to them, and this is still the case today.

The Changing Role of Soup
From playing the major part in almost every meal in every culture, the function of soups has changed dramatically and become almost reduced to a supporting role to the main course, an appetizer to set the scene for what is to come. Thus the majority of soups that are enjoyed today are thinner and less substantial than their illustrious ancestors, being lighter and less filling.

Pasta in Soup
The very nature of modern-day soups demands that you don't attempt to cook large pasta shells or spirals in them. They would look ungainly, be much larger than the majority of the other ingredients and would also be more than a little difficult to eat elegantly with a spoon! There are a great number of small pasta shapes available specifically for soups, which cook quickly and are easy to eat. These range from cartoon characters and alphabet letters (doubtless to encourage children to eat their food by making it fun) to tiny shells and other, more sophisticated shapes. As there is such a variety of

pasta for soup, most of the shapes do not have their own names but are known by the general term of *pastini* or *pasta in brodo*.

Quick to Cook

I feel that you would need the patience of a saint to fashion even a one-egg dough mix into pastini for soup! It is therefore much easier to buy these little pasta shapes in a dried form, and to keep them in reserve for use as required. As the shapes are so small, they are quick to cook – most dried pasta shapes have to be boiled for 10-12 minutes, but pastini are generally cooked within 4-5 minutes.

Two Classics from the Two Great Pasta Nations

China and Italy, the two great pasta nations, each have a classic pasta soup that is an integral part of their national cuisine. In Italy it is Minestrone, which would be little more than a tomato soup without the addition of broken spaghetti to help thicken the brew, while the classic Chicken Noodle is one of the most popular of Chinese soups. When made with a fresh and nutritious chicken stock, it provides an excellent light meal for invalids and those without much appetite.

Hearty Soups for Cold Winter Days

Most pasta soups are really throwbacks to the days of one-pot eating: they are richly flavored, hearty meals that almost have the consistency of a stew (although usually without meat), and can be served as a complete meal with the simple addition of a loaf of fresh, crusty bread. This chapter contains recipes from different countries, all of which feature pasta. The Spiced Fried Soup is a classic dish from Indonesia, whereas the Cabbage and Pasta Soup is based on the French passion for cabbage dishes.

Surprise Packages in the Soup

No, not a repetition of "Waiter, there's a fly in my soup!" I am referring to the tradition of serving more substantial mouthfuls in a well-flavored stock or consommé, in the same way as the Chinese would serve a wonton soup with little savory packages in a clear broth. I have included recipes for Ravioli Soup, the Italian answer to the Chinese wonton dish which is served in a tomato-flavored stock, and a Meatball Soup, which includes baked meatballs in a tasty liquor containing pastini.

MINESTRONE

There are so many recipes for the classic Italian soup of minestrone. This recipe has a rich, pesto-like mayonnaise added as a delicious garnish.

Serves 4-6

INGREDIENTS
⅔ cup dried navy beans, soaked overnight
2 tablespoons olive oil
4-ounce piece bacon
1 carrot, diced
2 potatoes, diced
⅓ cup peas (shelled, fresh or frozen)
½ zucchini, diced
4 ounces pasta shells

Sauce
10 fresh basil leaves
1 tablespoon pine nuts
1 egg yolk
1 clove garlic, finely chopped
⅔ cup olive oil
Salt and freshly ground black pepper
¼ cup finely grated Cheddar or Parmesan cheese

Rinse and drain the beans. Heat the olive oil in a large saucepan, and fry the beans and bacon over a low heat for 1 minute. Add plenty of water, and cook for about 45 minutes until the beans are cooked.

To make the sauce, crush together the basil leaves and the pine nuts. Add the egg and garlic. Gradually whisk in the olive oil until the sauce thickens like mayonnaise. Season with salt and pepper. Add the grated cheese to the sauce; stir well, and set aside.

Add the carrot, potatoes and peas to the beans, cook for an additional 15 minutes, and, then add the zucchini and pasta and cook for a final 15 minutes. Remove the piece of bacon, and serve the soup accompanied by the sauce.

CHICKEN SOUP WITH VERMICELLI

This light chicken soup is perfect as part of a Mediterranean-style meal, but may also be used as a nutritious dish to tempt anyone who has lost their appetite.

Serves 4

INGREDIENTS
3 tablespoons butter
1 carrot, finely sliced
1 bay leaf
1 onion, finely sliced
2¼-pound chicken carcass
  (bones and meat)
½ leek (white part only), finely
  sliced
Salt and freshly ground black
  pepper
2 ounces vermicelli
2 tablespoons freshly chopped
  chives

Melt the butter, and gently fry the carrot and bay leaf for 2 minutes. Add the onion, and continue cooking for 2 minutes. Add the chicken carcass, roughly chopped, and fry, shaking the pan, for a few minutes. Pour over enough water to cover the ingredients. Stir in the leek, and season with salt and pepper. Cook over a medium heat for 45 minutes, adding extra water if necessary. Drain the contents of the pan through a fine strainer, reserving only the stock. Pour the stock into a clean saucepan. Bring to a boil, and add the vermicelli. Cook for approximately 2 minutes, then serve, sprinkled with the chopped chives.

CHICKEN AND VEGETABLE SOUP WITH CURRY

This spicy Thai recipe for chicken soup is delicious! Be careful when seasoning the soup – macadamia nuts can be very salty, and little or no extra seasoning may be required.

Serves 4

INGREDIENTS

2¼ pounds chicken pieces
1 tablespoon curry leaves
2 tablespoons oil
4 shallots, roughly chopped
1 clove garlic, crushed
1 red or green chili, seeded and finely chopped
2 teaspoons mild curry powder
1 small piece fresh gingerroot, grated
¼ cup chopped macadamia nuts

3 ounces Chinese noodles, softened for 5 minutes in hot water
2 zucchini, diced
Juice of 1 lime
Salt

Garnish
Thin slices of lime

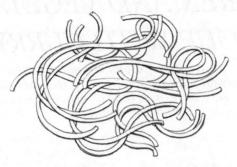

Put the chicken pieces and curry leaves into a deep pan, and cover with water. Simmer, partially covered, for 30-45 minutes, or until the chicken is tender. Skim the fat or scum from the top of the liquid while the chicken cooks.

Heat the oil in a small pan, and add the shallots and garlic. Cook until slightly softened. Add the chili, curry powder and gingerroot and cook for 2 minutes. Add the nuts, and set aside.

When the chicken is cooked, remove it from the liquid, and let cool. Strain and reserve the stock. Remove the skin and bones from the chicken, and cut the meat into small pieces. Add the chicken and cooked onions, garlic and spices to the strained stock in the rinsed-out pan. Bring to a boil, and add the noodles and zucchini. Simmer to cook the noodles completely, and add lime juice and salt, if necessary. Garnish with lime slices and serve.

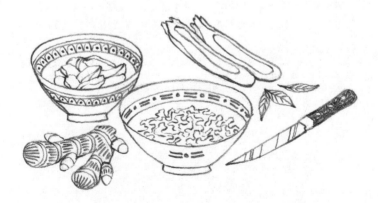

SPICED FRIED SOUP

This soup is so substantial that it is a complete meal in itself.
It is a classic dish of Indonesia.

Serves 4

INGREDIENTS
4-8 tablespoons oil
1 clove garlic
1-pound chicken breast, skinned,
  boned and cut into small
  pieces
8 ounces tofu, drained and cut
  into 1-inch cubes
½ cup raw cashew nuts
4 shallots, roughly chopped
1 carrot, very thinly sliced
3 ounces snow peas
2 ounces Chinese noodles,
  soaked for 5 minutes in hot
  water and drained thoroughly
3 pints vegetable or chicken
  stock
Juice of 1 lime
¼ teaspoon turmeric
2 curry leaves
1 teaspoon grated fresh
  gingerroot
1 tablespoon soy sauce
Salt and freshly ground black
  pepper

Heat 2-3 tablespoons of the oil in
a wok or large skillet. Add the
garlic, and cook until brown.
Remove the garlic from the pan,
and discard it. Add the chicken
pieces, and cook in the oil until
they begin to brown. Remove the
pieces using a draining spoon,
and drain well on paper towels.
Add a little more oil, and cook
the tofu until lightly brown.
Remove and drain well. Add the
cashews, and cook, stirring
constantly, until toasted. Remove
and drain well. Add a little more
oil, and fry the shallots and
carrots until lightly browned. Stir
in the snow peas and cook for 1
minute. Remove from the pan,
and drain.

Heat the oil in the wok until it is
very hot, adding any remaining
from the original amount. Add
the drained noodles, and cook
quickly until brown on one side.
Turn over, and brown the other
side. Lower the heat, and pour in
the stock. Stir in the lime juice,
turmeric, curry leaves,
gingerroot, soy sauce and
seasoning. Cover and simmer
gently for 10 minutes, stirring
occasionally to prevent the
noodles from sticking. Add the
fried ingredients, and heat
through for 5 minutes. Season to
taste, and serve immediately.

LAMB AND NOODLE SOUP

Most Chinese soups are light and thin, but this one is quite substantial. Slice the lamb very thinly to insure that it cooks through quickly. Cellophane noodles may be cut with a sharp knife if they are difficult to break.

Serves 4

INGREDIENTS

4 ounces cellophane noodles
6 Chinese dried mushrooms, soaked for 15 minutes in warm water
3 cups lamb stock, skimmed
6 ounces lamb tenderloin, thinly sliced
1 tablespoon soy sauce
Few drops of chili sauce
Salt and freshly ground black pepper

Break the cellophane noodles into small pieces, and cook them in boiling, salted water for 20 seconds. Rinse them in fresh water, and set aside to drain. Cook the mushrooms in boiling, lightly salted water for 15 minutes; then rinse in fresh water, and set aside to drain. Cut the mushrooms into thin slices.

Heat the lamb stock in a saucepan, and add the lamb, mushrooms, soy sauce and a few drops of chili sauce. Season with salt and pepper, and simmer gently for 15 minutes. Stir in the drained noodles, and simmer for just long enough for the noodles to heat through. Serve immediately.

BEEF AND NOODLE SOUP

This is a rich, filling soup, deliciously flavored with marinated beef.

Serves 4

INGREDIENTS
8 ounces beef fillet
1 clove garlic, chopped
1 scallion, chopped
2 tablespoons soy sauce
Salt and freshly ground black
    pepper
8 ounces fresh noodles or fine
    tagliatelle
Few drops of sesame oil
3 cups beef stock
Few drops of chili sauce
1 tablespoon freshly chopped
    chives

Cut the beef into thin slices. Sprinkle the chopped garlic and scallion over the meat with the soy sauce, and season with salt and pepper. Marinate the meat for 15 minutes. Cook the noodles in boiling, salted water, to which a few drops of sesame oil have been added, until tender but still firm. Rinse the noodles, and set aside to drain. Bring the beef stock to a boil, and add the beef and the marinade. Simmer gently for 10 minutes. Stir in the noodles. Season with a few drops of chili sauce, and simmer for just long enough to heat the noodles through. Serve garnished with chives.

THICK CHICKEN NOODLE SOUP

A very meaty and substantial soup. Add more water or stock for a thinner and less filling soup.

Serves 6

INGREDIENTS
1 chicken weighing about 3
   pounds
2 carrots, chopped
1 leek, sliced
2 ounces vermicelli noodles
1 tablespoon freshly chopped
   mixed herbs
Salt and freshly ground black
   pepper

Cut the chicken into pieces, and put into a large pan with sufficient water to cover the meat. Add the chopped vegetables, and bring to a boil. Cover the pan, and simmer for 1 hour.

Strain the liquid, and return it to the pan. Bone the chicken, shred the meat, and return it to the pan. Bring to a boil, and add the vermicelli, herbs and seasonings. Simmer for an additional 15 minutes, adding extra water if necessary. Season to taste, and serve.

GARBANZO BEAN SOUP

This is a substantial soup, suitable for the coldest of winter days. Liquidize the soup before adding the pasta, if preferred.

Serves 4

INGREDIENTS
Generous 1 cup dried garbanzo
  beans
3 tablespoons olive oil
2 cloves garlic
12-ounce can chopped plum
  tomatoes
3 cups water
1 tablespoon fresh basil leaves
1 chicken bouillon cube
Salt and freshly ground black
  pepper
5 ounces small pasta shapes for
  soup
⅓ cup grated Parmesan cheese

Soak the garbanzo beans overnight in enough water to cover them by 1 inch. Discard the water and put the beans in a large, heavy pan with a similar amount of fresh water. Bring to a boil, and simmer, covered, for about 1 hour, until the beans are tender, insuring that they do not boil dry.

Heat the olive oil in a heavy pan, and sauté the garlic cloves. When browned, remove and discard the garlic. Add the tomatoes and their juice, the water and basil, and cook for 20 minutes. Add the drained beans, crumbled bouillon cube, and salt and pepper to taste. Stir well, and simmer for an additional 10 minutes.

Return the soup to a boil, and add the pasta, then cook, stirring frequently, for 10 minutes. Mix in half of the Parmesan cheese. Adjust the seasoning, and serve immediately, with the remaining Parmesan cheese sprinkled on top.

CABBAGE AND PASTA SOUP

Cabbage soups are very popular in France, but this one has a very definite Italian flavor.

Serves 4

INGREDIENTS
6 leaves white cabbage
5 ounces small pasta shells
1 slice bacon, cut into small dice
1 clove garlic, chopped
1 tablespoon olive oil
3½ cups chicken stock
Salt and freshly ground black
  pepper

Cut the cabbage into thin shreds. To do this, roll the leaves into cigar shapes, and cut with a very sharp knife. Heat the olive oil in a large pan, and fry the garlic, bacon and cabbage together for 2 minutes. Add the stock, and season with salt and pepper. Cook over a medium heat for 30 minutes. Add the pasta to the soup after it has been cooking for 15 minutes. Check the seasoning, and serve.

TOMATO SOUP

A tomato soup with a difference. Use two tablespoons of horseradish sauce if grated horseradish is not available.

Serves 4-6

Ingredients

2 tablespoons butter or margarine
1 small onion, chopped
1 small green bell pepper, seeded and chopped
1 tablespoon all-purpose flour
4½ cups brown stock, or water plus 2 beef bouillon cubes
1 pound tomatoes, chopped
2 tablespoons tomato paste
Salt and freshly ground black pepper
4 ounces short-cut macaroni
1 tablespoon grated horseradish

Garnish

2 tablespoons sour cream
1 tablespoon freshly chopped parsley

Melt the butter or margarine in a pan, add the onion and green bell pepper, then cover and cook for 5 minutes. Add the flour and stir. Cook for 1 minute, then add the stock, tomatoes and tomato paste. Bring to a boil, then simmer for 15 minutes.

Purée the soup until smooth in a blender or food processor, then press it through a strainer. Return it to the pan, and season with salt and pepper to taste. Add the macaroni 10 minutes before serving. Simmer and stir occasionally. Stir in the horseradish, and garnish with sour cream and parsley. Serve immediately.

BEAN SOUP

Not so much a soup, more a meal in a dish!

Serves 4-6

INGREDIENTS
15-ounce can red kidney beans
⅓ cup chopped, rindless bacon
1 stalk celery, chopped
1 small onion, chopped
1 clove garlic, crushed
1 tablespoon freshly chopped
  parsley
1 tablespoon freshly chopped
  basil
½ cup seeded and chopped
  canned plum tomatoes
4½ cups water
1 chicken bouillon cube
Salt and freshly ground black
  pepper
4 ounces whole wheat pasta

Put the kidney beans, bacon, celery, onion, garlic, parsley, basil, tomatoes and water into a large pan. Bring to a boil, and add the bouillon cube and salt and pepper to taste. Cover and simmer for about 1½ hours. Return the soup to a boil, and add the pasta, stirring well. Stir frequently until the pasta is cooked but still firm – about 10 minutes. Season and serve immediately.

SHRIMP AND NOODLE SOUP

This is a hearty, satisfying fish soup. The tofu provides plenty of protein and makes the soup almost a complete meal in itself.

Serves 4

INGREDIENTS
1 small bunch scallions
1½ cups raw, unshelled shrimp
1 bay leaf
1 small piece fresh gingerroot, peeled and left whole
2 cloves garlic, peeled and left whole
1 tablespoon crushed coriander seeds
4½ cups water
¼ teaspoon turmeric
1 red chili, seeded and cut into very thin, short strips
1¼ cups coconut milk
6 ounces Chinese noodles, soaked for 5 minutes in hot water
8 ounces tofu, drained and cut into ½-inch cubes
3 cups bean sprouts
Lemon juice
Salt

Cut the green tops off the scallions and set aside. Combine the white part of the scallions, shrimp, bay leaf, gingerroot, garlic, coriander seeds and water in a deep saucepan. Bring to a boil, and simmer just until the shrimp turn pink. Remove the shrimp with a draining spoon and, shell them. Return the shells to the stock in the pan. Chop the shrimp, and set them aside. Simmer the stock for an additional 15-20 minutes. Strain and return to the rinsed-out pan. Add the turmeric, chili and coconut milk. Bring to a boil, add the noodles and simmer until completely cooked. Slice the green tops of the scallions thinly, and add to the stock with the tofu, bean sprouts, lemon juice and shrimp. Add salt to taste, and simmer until all the ingredients are hot.

CURRIED MEATBALL AND NOODLE SOUP

Oriental noodle soups often contain meatballs. Chop the shallots for the meatballs very finely to prevent the meatballs from breaking up during cooking.

Serves 4

INGREDIENTS

Meatballs
2 cups finely ground lean beef
2 shallots, finely chopped
Pinch of salt and pepper
1 teaspoon cornstarch
1 egg white

Soup
2 tablespoons oil
3 shallots, finely chopped
1 clove garlic, crushed
1 tablespoon curry powder
1 carrot, peeled and sliced
3 pints stock
Salt and freshly ground black pepper
3 ounces Chinese noodles
Half a head bok-choi, shredded

Garnish
Chopped macadamia nuts
Cilantro leaves

Combine all the ingredients for the meatballs, and mix well. Shape into 1-inch balls, and chill until ready to use.

Heat the oil in a heavy-bottomed saucepan, and add the shallots, garlic and curry powder. Cook until the shallots soften. Add the carrots and stock. Partially cover the pan, and bring the stock to a boil. Let simmer for 15 minutes, then add the meatballs. Simmer for 5-7 minutes, or until the meatballs are cooked. Add the Chinese noodles, and cook about 5 minutes or until just tender. Add salt, pepper and the bok-choi. Cook for an additional 5 minutes until the leaves are tender-crisp. Spoon the soup into individual bowls, and garnish with chopped nuts and whole cilantro leaves.

MINESTRA

*This is a substantial variation on the classic Italian soup
Minestrone. I particularly like the spinach in it.*

Serves 4-6

INGREDIENTS
1 onion
1 carrot
1 stalk celery
2 tablespoons olive oil
3½ pints water
Salt and freshly ground black
  pepper
8 ounces fresh spinach
2 tomatoes
4 ounces short-cut macaroni
2 cloves garlic, crushed
2 tablespoons freshly chopped
  parsley
1 teaspoon freshly chopped
  rosemary
½ cup grated Parmesan cheese

Cut the onion, carrot and celery
into thick matchsticks. Heat the
oil in a large, heavy pan, and fry
the vegetable strips until just
browning, stirring occasionally.
Add the water, salt and pepper,
and simmer for 20 minutes.
Meanwhile, wash the spinach
leaves, and cut them into shreds.
Add to the soup, and cook for 10
minutes. Peel the tomatoes, and
chop them roughly, removing the
seeds. Add the tomatoes,
macaroni, garlic, parsley and
rosemary to the soup, and
simmer for an additional 10
minutes. Adjust the seasoning.
Serve with grated Parmesan
cheese.

RAVIOLI SOUP

The ravioli makes surprise packages of flavor in a clear soup.
The secret of success is to use a good homemade stock.

Serves 4

INGREDIENTS
8 ounces pasta dough (see page
    19)
3 slices prosciutto, cut into very
    thin strips
4½ cups chicken stock
2 tablespoons butter
1 egg, beaten
1 sprig tarragon, leaves stripped
    off and cut into thin strips
2 tablespoons light cream
Nutmeg
Salt and freshly ground black
    pepper

Prepare the pasta dough, and roll
it out very thinly, either with a
rolling pin or by passing it
through a pasta machine. Cut it
into rectangles. Put a little
Prosciutto and butter on one half
of each piece, then brush the
edges of the dough with the
beaten egg. Fold each rectangle
in half to form a square, and
pinch the edges well with your
fingers to seal. Cut into neat
squares or various shapes using a
ravioli cutter, and pinch the
edges to seal, if necessary.

Bring the stock to a boil, and
season with nutmeg, salt and
pepper. Add the ravioli to the
stock, and cook for about 2-5
minutes, depending on the
thickness of the ravioli. They will
float when cooked. Stir the cream
into the soup just before serving,
and sprinkle with the tarragon.
Serve hot.

GLASS NOODLE SOUP

Don't worry about the name of this soup! The glass noodles are cellophane noodles, and the soup also contains tasty chicken meatballs.

Serves 4

INGREDIENTS
2 tablespoons oil
2 cloves garlic, thinly sliced
2 ounces dried cellophane
   noodles
8 ounces skinned and boneless
   chicken breast
2 tablespoons green curry paste
2 tablespoons fish sauce
3 tablespoons cornstarch
1 tablespoon freshly chopped
   cilantro
4½ pints chicken stock
8 ounces bok-choi, shredded
4 scallions, cut into 1-inch pieces

Heat the oil in a small skillet or wok, and fry the garlic until golden. Remove with a draining spoon, and drain on paper towels.

Put the noodles into a large bowl, and cover with hot water. Let soak until softened, then drain.

Dice the chicken, and put into a food processor with the curry paste, fish sauce, cornstarch and cilantro. Process until very finely ground. Remove the mixture from the processor, and shape into small balls. Heat the stock in a large saucepan until boiling, and add the balls. Cook for 10-15 minutes, or until they rise to the surface. Add the softened noodles, bok-choi and scallions, and continue cooking for 5 minutes. Serve garnished with the fried garlic slices.

THAI BEEF SOUP

This soup recipe uses egg noodles, but you could ring the changes by using cellophane or rice noodles. This delicious Thai recipe is an excellent dinner party soup.

Serves 4

INGREDIENTS
2 tablespoons oil
8 ounces sirloin steak, cut into thin strips
1 small onion, chopped
2 stalks celery, sliced diagonally
3 pints beef stock
1 tablespoon freshly chopped cilantro
2 kaffir lime leaves
1-inch piece fresh gingerroot, peeled and thinly sliced
1 teaspoon palm sugar
1 tablespoon fish sauce
3 ounces egg noodles
½ cup drained, canned straw mushrooms

Heat the oil in a wok or saucepan, and fry the meat, onion and celery until the meat is cooked through and the vegetables are soft. Add the stock, cilantro, lime leaves, gingerroot, sugar and fish sauce. Bring to a boil; then add the noodles and straw mushrooms, and cook for 10 minutes. Serve piping hot.

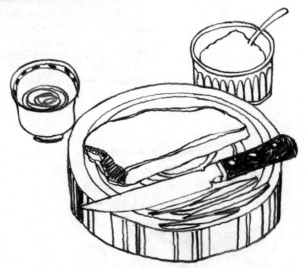

MEATBALL SOUP

A satisfying soup for a cold winter's day. I prefer to cook the meatballs separately in the oven as they keep a better shape and texture than if they are boiled.

Serves 4

INGREDIENTS
1 pound beef bones
1 carrot, chopped
1 onion, chopped
1 stalk celery, chopped
1 egg, beaten
2 cups ground beef
1 cup bread crumbs
Salt and freshly ground black
   pepper
1 tablespoon oil
15-ounce can plum tomatoes
6 ounce small pasta shapes for
   soup
1 tablespoon freshly chopped
   parsley

Preheat the oven to 375°. Put the bones, carrot, onion and celery into a large saucepan, and cover with cold water. Bring to a boil, then cover and simmer for 1½ hours. Meanwhile, mix together the lightly beaten egg, ground beef, bread crumbs and plenty of seasoning. Roll the mixture into small balls about the size of walnuts, and put into a roasting pan with the oil. Bake pan for 45 minutes, turning occasionally.

Strain the stock into a saucepan. Press the tomatoes and their juice through a strainer, and add to stock. Bring to a boil, and simmer for 15 minutes. Add the pasta to the stock, and cook for 10 minutes, stirring frequently. Add the meatballs. Adjust the seasoning, and stir in the chopped parsley. Serve hot.

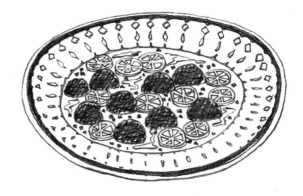

PASTA WITH VEGETABLES

Although many of the great classic pasta dishes feature meat or fish in a sauce, I find that vegetables make a perfect partnership with pasta. Providing that you have the ingredients to make fresh pasta or a package of dried, some fresh vegetables and butter or olive oil, you have the basis of a sustaining, tasty and nutritious meal.

Pasta in the Vegetarian Diet

Pasta plays a valuable part in the diet of many vegetarians. If they eat eggs, vegetarians will enjoy fresh pasta, but, if not, the dried varieties do not contain egg and are therefore suitable for the stricter vegetarian diets. There are many recipes creating complicated meatless variations on the classic favorites of Bolognese sauce, lasagne and stuffed cannelloni, and they are delicious, relying on nuts, fresh herbs and vegetables such as spinach for their rich flavors. However, one vegetable fried until soft in butter or olive oil with a little garlic, and then mixed into freshly cooked pasta with plenty of black pepper and Parmesan cheese produces a sumptuous but simple meal. My favorite vegetable for cooking in this way is zucchini, and the recipe for Zucchini Spaghetti is a firm favorite in our house, especially in the late summer when zucchini are plentiful in the garden.

Pasta and Tomatoes – an Established Double Act

As Italy both produces and consumes vast quantities of tomatoes and pasta, it is inevitable that tomato sauces have become one of the most popular accompaniments for pasta. I wonder just how many different recipes there are for tomato sauce? I think that an essential ingredient is fresh basil, a herb that just seems to have been invented to flavor tomatoes, but I also like to add eggs and freshly grated Parmesan if the dish of pasta and tomato sauce is to be the main meal of the day. When adding basil to sauces, I find that a better flavor is obtained if the leaves are torn and not chopped – basil bruises easily and the flavor can become musty. The recipe for Tagliatelle with Rich Tomato Sauce is one of my favorites.

Pasta and Mushrooms – Dried or Fresh

Made into a sauce or served sliced, mushrooms are also an excellent choice to serve with pasta. Dried mushrooms, especially the Italian porcini, give a very strong flavor and make an excellent seasoning for any pasta dish, but I actually like to use a mixture of dried and fresh mushrooms for most dishes – I almost find dried mushrooms too overwhelming by themselves. Many people soak dried mushrooms in boiling water, but I like to soak them in sherry and then to use it as part of the sauce – I use a medium sherry, and it certainly adds an extra dimension to most mushroom dishes! However, you will need to leave the mushrooms to soak for at least an hour – soaking in boiling water gives much quicker results, but I prefer the flavor achieved by the slower soaking!

Pasta and Vegetable Salads

Cold cooked pasta and crisp vegetables make excellent salads, to serve either as main courses or as part of a buffet. There are many ideas for pasta salads in this chapter, and they can be sophisticated dishes or hearty, family fare. I particularly like the green pasta salad with avocados, either as a supper dish or as an appetizer when entertaining. Pasta salads can be made more filling by adding cheese, but I often do this in the form of a cheese dressing, which gives a better, all-round blend of flavors. A blue cheese dressing on a pasta and avocado salad is high on my list of delectable dishes!

Chinese Noodles and Seasonings

The Chinese, who, like the Italians, are also great pasta eaters, often make fragrant dishes of thin egg noodles, served in a gravy-like sauce richly flavored with such fragrant ingredients as fresh gingerroot and sesame oil. If a number of vegetables are braised slowly in the sauce, and freshly cooked noodles are mixed in just before serving, you have a splendid dish which simply requires an accompaniment of crispy stir-fried vegetables to be served with it. Five-Colored Noodles is an excellent Chinese recipe for noodles and vegetables, and, incidentally, it's the vegetable garnish and not the noodles themselves that are five-colored!

Just a few vegetables and a package of pasta form the basic ingredients for so many dishes – the following is but a small selection of recipes, and you will be able to create many more of your own.

STUFFED TOMATOES

Use large, beefsteak tomatoes for this recipe – it is an ideal appetizer.

Serves 4

INGREDIENTS
4 large ripe tomatoes
1 pound fresh spinach
2 ounces small pasta shapes for soup
2 tablespoons softened butter
1 tablespoon heavy cream
¼ teaspoon grated nutmeg
1 clove garlic, crushed
Salt and freshly ground black pepper
1 tablespoons grated Parmesan or Cheddar cheese
4 anchovy fillets, halved lengthwise

Preheat the oven to 400°F. Cut the tops off the tomatoes, and carefully scoop out the insides with a teaspoon. Wash the spinach well, and remove the stalks. Cook the spinach slowly in a large saucepan, without added water, until it is soft. Chop the spinach very finely, or purée in a blender or food processor. Squeeze to remove excess moisture.

Meanwhile, cook the pasta in boiling water for 5 minutes, or until *al dente*. Rinse and drain well, then mix with the spinach. Add the butter, cream, nutmeg and garlic, and season well. Fill each tomato, and top with the cheese and anchovies. Bake for 10 minutes. Serve immediately.

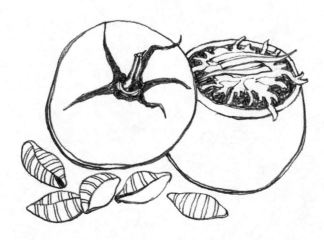

STUFFED ZUCCHINI

Stuffed zucchini make an elegant appetizer – be certain to choose same size zucchini for this dish.

Serves 4

INGREDIENTS

2 ounces small pasta shapes for soup
4 zucchini
2 tablespoons butter or margarine
2 cloves garlic, crushed
1 small onion, chopped
1 cup ground beef
1 teaspoon tomato paste
Salt and freshly ground black pepper
2 tomatoes, peeled, chopped and seeds removed
½ cup grated fontina cheese
1 tablespoon fresh bread crumbs

Cook the pasta in plenty of boiling, salted water for 5 minutes, or until tender. Rinse in cold water, and drain well. Meanwhile, put the zucchini into a pan, and cover with cold water. Bring to a boil, and cook over a low heat for 3 minutes. Rinse under cold water. Cut the zucchini in half lengthwise, and carefully scoop out the pulp, leaving a ½-inch shell. Chop the pulp.

Melt the butter or margarine in a skillet. Add the garlic and onion, and fry slowly until transparent. Increase the heat, and add the ground beef. Fry for 5 minutes, stirring frequently, until the meat is well browned. Stir in the tomato paste and salt and pepper to taste. Add the zucchini pulp, tomatoes and pasta, and cook for 2 minutes. Spoon the mixture into the zucchini shells, and top with the grated cheese and bread crumbs. Brown under a broiler or in a hot oven. Serve immediately.

STUFFED EGGPLANTS

Eggplants are very underrated in my opinion. Baking brings out their sweet flavor.

Serves 4

INGREDIENTS
2 ounces macaroni
4 small or 2 large eggplants
2 tablespoons butter
1 small onion, chopped
1 clove garlic, crushed
1½ cups diced rindless, bacon
1 green bell pepper, seeded and diced
1 yellow bell pepper, seeded and diced
2 tomatoes, peeled, chopped and seeds removed
1 tablespoon tomato paste
½ teaspoon chili powder
Salt and freshly ground black pepper
½ cup grated Mozzarella cheese
1 tablespoon fresh bread crumbs

Preheat the oven to 375°F. Cook the macaroni in plenty of boiling, salted water for 10 minutes, or until tender but still firm. Rinse in cold water, and drain well. Wrap the eggplants in foil, and bake for 30 minutes. Cut the eggplants in half lengthwise. Scoop out the pulp, leaving a ½-inch shell, and chop the pulp.

Melt the butter in a pan. Add the onion and garlic, and cook until soft and transparent. Add the bacon and bell peppers, and fry for 5 minutes, then add the eggplant pulp, tomatoes, tomato paste, chili powder, and salt and pepper. Cook for an additional 3 minutes. Stir in the macaroni, and fill the scooped-out eggplant halves with the mixture. Top with the grated cheese and bread crumbs, and brown under a preheated broiler or in the oven set at 400°F. Serve immediately.

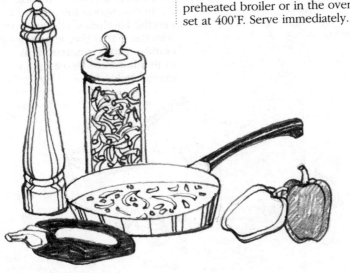

ZUCCHINI AND PINE NUT LASAGNE WITH EGGPLANT SAUCE

Not all lasagnes are made with a meat sauce – this delicious variation is light and fragrant. It is a perfect vegetarian dinner party dish.

Serves 4

INGREDIENTS
12 sheets of whole wheat lasagne
¾ cup pine nuts
2 tablespoons butter
1½ pounds zucchini, trimmed and sliced
1¼ cups ricotta cheese
½ teaspoon nutmeg
1 tablespoon olive oil
1 large eggplant, sliced
⅔ cup water
Salt and freshly ground black pepper
¾ cup grated Cheddar cheese

Preheat the oven to 375°F. Cook the lasagne in plenty of boiling, salted water for 8-10 minutes, then drain and leave on clean dishcloths until required. Put the pine nuts into a dry pan, and roast over a low heat for 2 minutes. Set aside. Melt the butter, and cook the zucchini, with a little water if necessary, until just tender. Combine the zucchini, pine nuts and ricotta cheese. Add the nutmeg, and mix thoroughly.

Heat the olive oil in a separate pan, and cook the eggplant for 4 minutes. Add the water, and simmer, covered, until soft. Season with salt and pepper. Purée in a blender or food processor until smooth, adding a little extra water if necessary. Put 4 sheets of lasagne in the bottom of a greased, ovenproof dish, and top with half the zucchini mixture. Put 4 strips of lasagne over the zucchini, and add half the eggplant sauce, followed by the remaining zucchini. Cover with the remaining lasagne and the remaining sauce. Top with the grated cheese, and bake for 40 minutes, until the cheese is golden-brown.

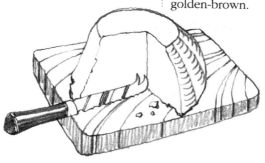

PASTA WITH BASIL AND TOMATO SAUCE

Use fully ripened tomatoes for this recipe; otherwise the sauce will be bland. If your fresh tomatoes are very green, you will achieve better results with canned tomatoes.

Serves 4

INGREDIENTS
1 pound pasta, any shape
3 tablespoons olive oil
1 clove garlic, chopped
3 tomatoes, peeled, seeded and chopped
Salt and freshly ground black pepper
10 fresh basil leaves, finely chopped

Cook the pasta in plenty of boiling, salted water. Rinse under hot water, and set aside to drain. Heat the olive oil in a skillet, and cook the garlic and tomato with a little salt and pepper over a low heat for about 12 minutes, stirring frequently. Stir the well drained pasta into the sauce. Mix together well, and heat through. Just before serving stir in the finely chopped basil, then check and adjust the seasoning. Serve hot.

PASTA SHELLS WITH MUSHROOM SAUCE

This tasty mushroom sauce poured over pasta makes a perfect lunch dish. I sometimes add a pinch of ground mace to the sauce – add it to the mushrooms while they are cooking.

Serves 4

INGREDIENTS

8 ounces button mushrooms
2 tablespoons butter or
  margarine
¼ cup all-purpose flour
2½ cups milk
Salt and freshly ground black
  pepper
10 ounces pasta shells

Rinse the mushrooms, and chop them roughly. Melt the butter or margarine in a saucepan, and add the mushrooms. Fry for 5 minutes, stirring occasionally. Stir in the flour, and cook for 1 minute.

Take the pan off the heat, and add the milk gradually, stirring continuously. Return to the heat and bring to a boil, then cook for 3 minutes, stirring continuously. Season with salt and pepper.

Meanwhile, cook the pasta shells in plenty of boiling, salted water for 10 minutes, or until *al dente*. Rinse in hot water, and drain well. Put into a warmed serving dish, and add the mushroom sauce. Serve immediately.

ZUCCHINI SALAD

I think raw zucchini are nicer than cooked ones! They make a wonderful pasta salad.

Serves 4

INGREDIENTS
8 ounces macaroni
4 tomatoes
4-5 zucchini, thinly sliced
8 stuffed green olives, sliced
6 tablespoons French dressing
Salt and freshly ground black
  pepper

Cook the macaroni in a large pan of boiling, salted water for 10 minutes, or until tender but still firm. Rinse in cold water, and drain well.

Cut a small cross in the top of each tomato, and plunge them into boiling water for 30 seconds. Carefully remove the skins from the tomatoes, using a sharp knife. Chop the tomatoes roughly. Mix all the ingredients in a large bowl, and chill for 30 minutes before serving. Add extra salt and pepper if necessary.

MUSHROOM PASTA SALAD

Two of my favorite salads in one! Add a clove or two of crushed garlic if you wish.

Serves 4

INGREDIENTS
5 tablespoons olive oil
Juice of 2 lemons
1 tablespoon freshly chopped basil
1 tablespoon freshly chopped parsley
Salt and freshly ground black pepper
2½ cups finely sliced mushrooms
8 ounces whole wheat pasta shapes of your choice

Whisk together the olive oil, lemon juice, herbs and seasonings in a large bowl. Add the sliced mushrooms to the lemon dressing, stirring well to coat the mushrooms evenly. Cover the bowl, and let marinate in a cool place for at least 1 hour.

Cook the pasta in a large pan of boiling, salted water for 10 minutes, or until just tender. Rinse the pasta in cold water, and drain well. Add the pasta to the marinated mushrooms and lemon dressing, mixing well to coat the pasta evenly. Adjust the seasoning if necessary, then chill well before serving.

GIANFOTTERE SALAD

A pasta salad which celebrates summer vegetables.

Serves 4

INGREDIENTS
1 small eggplant
2 tomatoes
1 large zucchini
1 red bell pepper
1 green bell pepper
1 onion
1 clove garlic
4 tablespoons olive oil
Freshly ground sea salt and black pepper
1 pound whole wheat pasta spirals or bows

Cut the eggplant into ½-inch slices. Sprinkle with salt, and leave for 30 minutes. Chop the tomatoes roughly, and remove the woody cores. Cut the zucchini into ½-inch slices; then seed the bell peppers, and chop them roughly. Chop the onion, and crush the garlic.

Heat 3 tablespoons of the olive oil in a skillet, and cook the onion slowly until it is transparent but not colored. Rinse the salt from the eggplant thoroughly under running water, and pat dry with paper towels. Chop the eggplant roughly then stir it, with the zucchini, bell peppers, tomatoes and garlic, into the onion, and fry gently for 20 minutes. Season with salt and pepper to taste, and let cool completely.

Cook the pasta spirals in plenty of boiling, salted water for 10-15 minutes, or until tender. Rinse in cold water, and drain well. Put the pasta spirals into a large bowl, and stir in the remaining of olive oil. Stir the vegetables into the pasta, and season if necessary. Chill before serving.

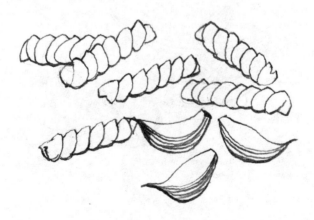

TORTIGLIONI ALLA PUTTANESCA

This is a well-flavored sauce, typical of many areas of central and southern Italy where strongly flavored ingredients such as chili, anchovies and garlic are popular.

Serves 4

INGREDIENTS
7-ounce can plum tomatoes, drained
2-ounce can anchovy fillets, drained
10 ounces tortiglioni, pasta spirals
2 tablespoons olive oil
1 clove garlic, crushed
Pinch of chili powder
4-5 fresh basil leaves, torn or chopped
2 tablespoons freshly chopped parsley
1 cup pitted and chopped black olives
Salt and freshly ground black pepper

Chop the tomatoes, and remove the seeds. Chop the anchovies. Cook the pasta in plenty of boiling salted water for 10 minutes, or until tender but still firm. Rinse in hot water, and drain well. Put into a warmed serving dish.

Meanwhile, heat the oil in a pan. Add the garlic and chili powder, and cook for 1 minute. Add the tomatoes, basil, parsley, olives and anchovies, and cook for a few minutes. Season with salt and pepper. Pour the sauce over the pasta, and mix together thoroughly. Serve immediately.

FRESH PASTA WITH CEPS

A wonderful recipe of intense flavor. Buy your ceps from a reliable mushroom supplier if you are unsure about gathering them yourself. Alternatively, use a mixture of fresh mushrooms if ceps are not available.

Serves 4

INGREDIENTS
1 pound fresh pasta
7 ounces ceps
⅓ cup butter
1-2 cloves garlic, chopped
Salt and freshly ground black
  pepper
1 tablespoon freshly chopped
  chives

Cook the pasta in boiling, salted water, until tender. Drain, rinse and set aside to drain. Cut off the stem ends from the ceps. Wash the mushrooms carefully, and dry them well; then cut into very thin slices. Melt one-third of the butter, and sauté the ceps with the garlic for 2 minutes. Season with plenty of salt and pepper. Add the remaining butter to the pan. When it has melted, add the pasta, and stir briskly; then add the chives. Cook until the pasta is heated through completely, and serve on warmed plates.

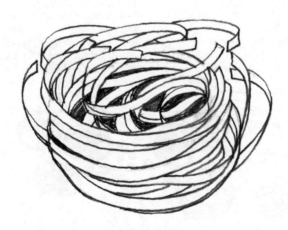

FETTUCCINE ESCARGOTS WITH LEEKS AND SUN-DRIED TOMATOES

Canned snails are delicious in dishes such as this, where they are flavored with garlic, mushrooms and dried tomatoes.

Serves 4-6

INGREDIENTS
6 sun-dried tomatoes
14-ounce can escargots (snails), drained
12 ounces fresh or dried whole wheat fettuccine (tagliatelle)
3 tablespoons olive oil
2 cloves garlic, crushed
1 large or 2 small leeks, trimmed and finely sliced
6 oyster, shiitake or other large mushrooms, sliced
4 tablespoons chicken or vegetable stock
3 tablespoons dry white wine
6 tablespoons heavy cream
1 tablespoon freshly chopped basil
1 tablespoon freshly chopped parsley
Salt and freshly ground black pepper

Chop the sun-dried tomatoes roughly. Drain the escargots well, and dry on paper towels.

Put the fettuccine into boiling, salted water, and cook for about 10-12 minutes, or until *al dente*. Drain, rinse under hot water, and leave in a colander to drain again. Meanwhile, heat the olive oil in a skillet, and add the garlic and leeks. Cook slowly until just starting to soften; then add the mushrooms, and cook until the leeks are just slightly crisp. Transfer the vegetables to a plate. Add the drained escargots to the pan, and cook over a high heat for about 2 minutes, stirring continuously. Add the stock and wine, and bring to a boil. Boil to reduce by about a quarter, then add the cream and the chopped sun-dried tomatoes. Bring to a boil, then cook slowly for about 3 minutes. Add the herbs, and salt and pepper to taste. Add the leeks, mushrooms and fettuccine to the pan, and heat through. Serve immediately.

PASTA PAPRIKA

This is pasta served in the style of a goulash, with plenty of bell peppers, tomato and paprika for seasoning.

Serves 4

INGREDIENTS

12 ounces green or wholewheat fettuccine, fresh or dried
1 teaspoon sunflower oil
1 tablespoon olive oil
1 large onion, chopped
1 clove garlic, crushed
2 teaspoons paprika
3 small bell peppers, one green, one red and one yellow, seeded and sliced
2½ cups passata (strained tomato purée)
Salt and freshly ground black pepper
½ cup grated Parmesan cheese

Put the pasta into a large pan of boiling, salted water, and add the sunflower oil. Cook for 8-15 minutes until the pasta is tender. Dried pasta will take longer to cook than fresh. Drain the cooked pasta while preparing the sauce.

Heat the olive oil, and fry the onion, garlic, paprika and sliced bell peppers for about 8 minutes until softened. Add the passata, and mix well. Add the vegetables and sauce mixture to the pasta, and stir well, then season to taste. Return the mixture to a large saucepan, and heat through slowly for 5 minutes. Serve immediately, topped with Parmesan cheese.

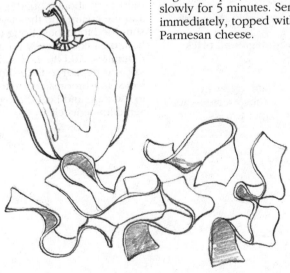

FARFALLE WITH TOMATO SAUCE

Tomato sauce is a favorite with any type of pasta.

Serves 2

INGREDIENTS
1 tablespoon olive oil
2 cloves garlic, crushed
1 onion, sliced
1 tablespoon fresh basil leaves, roughly torn
2 14-ounce cans plum tomatoes, chopped
Salt and freshly ground black pepper
10 ounces farfalle (pasta bows)
2 tablespoons freshly chopped basil or parsley
Grated Parmesan cheese

Heat the oil in a deep pan. Add the garlic and onion, and cook until softened. Add the torn basil, and cook for 30 seconds; then add the undrained tomatoes, and season with salt and pepper. Bring to a boil; then reduce the heat, and simmer, uncovered, for about 20 minutes, or until the sauce is reduced by half.

Meanwhile, cook the pasta in a large pan of boiling, salted water until tender but still firm – about 10 minutes. Rinse in hot water, and drain well. Press the sauce through a strainer, and stir in the fresh parsley or basil. Toss the sauce through the pasta. Serve immediately with grated Parmesan cheese.

SPINACH LASAGNE

Easy-cook lasagne is available, but it doesn't taste as good or cook as tenderly as that which you boil before baking.

Serves 4

INGREDIENTS
8 sheets green lasagne

Spinach sauce
¼ cup butter or margarine
½ cup all-purpose flour
1¼ cups milk
2 cups finely chopped, thawed
  frozen spinach
Pinch of ground nutmeg
Salt and freshly ground black
  pepper

Mornay sauce
2 tablespoons butter or
  margarine
¼ cup all-purpose flour
1¼ cups milk
¾ cup grated Parmesan cheese
1 teaspoon French mustard
Salt

To make the spinach sauce, melt the butter or margarine in a pan; then stir in the flour, and cook for 30 seconds. Take the pan off the heat, and gradually stir in the milk. Return to the heat, and bring to a boil, stirring continuously. Cook for 3 minutes, then add the spinach, nutmeg, and salt and pepper to taste. Set aside until needed.

Preheat the oven to 400°F. Cook the spinach lasagne in plenty of boiling, salted water for 10 minutes, or until tender. Rinse in cold water, and drain carefully. Dry on a clean cloth. To make the mornay sauce, melt the butter in a pan, and stir in the flour, cooking for 30 seconds. Remove from the heat, and stir in the milk. Return to the heat, stirring continuously, until boiling. Continue stirring, and simmer for 3 minutes. Add the mustard, two-thirds of the cheese, and salt to taste. Set aside until needed.

Grease an ovenproof baking dish. Line the base with a layer of lasagne, followed by some of the spinach mixture, and a layer of cheese sauce. Repeat the process, finishing with a layer of lasagne and a covering of the cheese sauce. Scatter the remaining cheese over the lasagne. Bake until golden, about 20-30 minutes. Serve immediately.

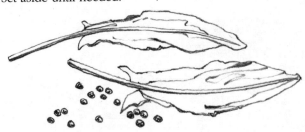

CANNELLONI WITH TOMATO AND CHEESE

*A filling of cheese and tomato, flavored with basil, makes this
a popular dish with vegetarians and
meat-eaters alike.*

Serves 4

INGREDIENTS
12 cannelloni shells

Filling
14-ounce can plum tomatoes
½ cup ricotta cheese
1 teaspoon tomato paste
1 tablespoon freshly chopped
  basil
1 cup grated Parmesan cheese
Salt and freshly ground black
  pepper

Sauce
1 tablespoon olive oil
1 onion, chopped
14-ounce can plum tomatoes
1 tablespoon cornstarch
Salt and freshly ground black
  pepper
¼ cup grated Parmesan cheese

Cook the cannelloni shells in a
large pan of boiling salted water
for 15-20 minutes, until tender.
Rinse in hot water, and drain
well. Chop the tomatoes for the
filling, and remove the seeds.

Set the juice aside for the sauce.
Beat the ricotta cheese until
smooth; then add the tomato
paste, basil and Parmesan
cheese, and beat well. Stir in the
chopped tomato, and salt and
pepper to taste. Fill the
cannelloni shells with a teaspoon
or a piping bag with a wide,
plain tip. Put into a greased
ovenproof dish.

Heat the oil for the sauce in a
pan, and cook the onion slowly
until transparent. Press the
tomatoes and their juice through
a strainer into the saucepan. Mix
the cornstarch with the reserved
tomato juice, and add it to the
pan. Bring to a boil, and cook for
3 minutes, stirring continuously.
Add salt and pepper to taste.
Pour the sauce over the
cannelloni, and sprinkle with the
cheese. Put under a preheated
broiler for 10 minutes, until
heated through. Serve
immediately.

PASTA WITH TOMATO AND YOGURT SAUCE

I wonder how many recipes there are for tomato sauce? Serve this dish with the yogurt topping the sauce, or marbled through the tomato mixture just before it is added to the pasta.

Serves 4

INGREDIENTS

1 tablespoon butter or margarine
2 tablespoons all-purpose flour
⅔ cup beef stock
14-ounce can plum tomatoes
1 bay leaf
Sprig of thyme
Parsley stalks
10 ounces pasta shells
Salt and freshly ground black
  pepper
3 tablespoons yogurt

Melt the butter or margarine in a pan. Stir in the flour, and cook for about 1 minute; then add the stock gradually. Add the undrained tomatoes, bay leaf, thyme and parsley stalks, and season with salt and pepper. Bring to a boil, stirring continuously, then simmer for 30 minutes. Press the sauce through a strainer back into a clean pan. Adjust the seasoning, and reheat.

Meanwhile, cook the pasta in plenty of boiling salted water for 10 minutes, or until tender but still firm. Rinse in hot water, and drain well. Put into a warmed serving dish, and pour the tomato sauce over. Top with the yogurt. Serve immediately.

PASTA SPIRALS WITH PEAS AND TOMATOES

Peas are widely used in Italian cookery – they provide color and texture in this dish.

Serves 4

INGREDIENTS
10 ounces pasta spirals
2½ cups shelled peas
1 teaspoon sugar
¼ cup butter or margarine
1 tablespoon freshly chopped
  basil
14-ounce can chopped tomatoes
Salt and freshly ground black
  pepper

Cook the pasta spirals in plenty of boiling, salted water for 10 minutes, or until tender. Drain. Meanwhile, cook the peas in boiling water with a pinch of salt and a teaspoon of sugar. Melt the butter or margarine in a pan. Add the basil, and cook for 30 seconds. Add the tomatoes and their juice. When hot, add the pasta spirals, peas, and salt and pepper to taste. Toss together, and serve immediately.

SPAGHETTI NEAPOLITANA

This is one of the classic tomato sauces – simple but packed with flavor.

Serves 4

INGREDIENTS

2 14-ounce cans plum tomatoes
2 tablespoons olive oil
1 tablespoon freshly chopped oregano or marjoram
Salt and freshly ground black pepper
10 ounces spaghetti
2 tablespoons freshly chopped parsley
Grated Parmesan cheese

Press the undrained tomatoes through a strainer. Heat the oil in a pan. Add the oregano or marjoram, and cook for 30 seconds. Add the puréed tomatoes, and salt and pepper. Bring to a boil; then reduce the heat, and simmer, uncovered, for 20-30 minutes.

Meanwhile, cook the spaghetti in plenty of boiling, salted water for about 10 minutes, or until tender but still firm. Rinse under hot water, and drain well. Pour the tomato sauce over the spaghetti, and toss gently. Sprinkle with the parsley, and serve with Parmesan cheese.

SPINACH RAVIOLI

Spinach makes an unusual but tasty filling for this dish of ravioli.

Serves 4

INGREDIENTS
Dough
2¼ cups white bread flour
3 eggs, lightly beaten

Filling
1½ cups cooked spinach
2 tablespoons butter or
  margarine
¼ cup grated Parmesan cheese
Pinch of grated nutmeg
Salt and freshly ground black
  pepper
1 egg, beaten

Cheese Sauce
2 tablespoons butter or
  margarine
2 tablespoons all-purpose flour
1¼ cups milk
1 teaspoon French mustard
¼ cup grated Parmesan cheese

Prepare the filling. Chop the spinach, and heat it in a pan; then beat in the butter or margarine. Add the Parmesan cheese, nutmeg, salt and freshly ground black pepper to taste. Finally mix in the beaten egg. Set aside until required.

Prepare the dough by sifting the flour into a bowl; make a well in the center and add the eggs.

Work the flour and the eggs together with a spoon, and then knead by hand until a smooth dough is formed. Let rest for 15 minutes. Lightly flour a work surface, and roll out the dough thinly into a rectangle. Cut the dough in half. Shape the filling into small balls, and set them about 1½ inches apart on one half of the dough. Put the other half on top, and cut with a ravioli cutter or small cooky cutter. Seal the edges. Cook in batches in a large pan with plenty of boiling, salted water until tender – about 8 minutes. Remove the ravioli carefully with a draining spoon. Meanwhile, make the sauce.

Melt the butter in a pan. Add the flour, and cook for 30 seconds. Take the pan off the heat, and gradually add the milk. Bring to a boil, and simmer for 3 minutes, stirring continuously. Add the mustard and half the cheese, and seasoning to taste. Pour the sauce over the ravioli, and serve immediately with the remaining cheese sprinkled over the top.

SPINACH-STUFFED CANNELLONI

Mozzarella, spinach and ham is one of my favorite pizza toppings – it is also a delicious filling for cannelloni.

Serves 4

INGREDIENTS
12 cannelloni shells
¼ cup butter
8 ounces spinach, washed and finely shredded
3 slices ham, cut into thin strips
8 ounces mozzarella cheese, cut into small cubes
¼ cup all-purpose flour
1¼ cups milk
Pinch of nutmeg
Salt and freshly ground black pepper
⅓ cup grated Parmesan cheese

Preheat the oven to 400°F. Cook the cannelloni in boiling, salted water, removing them when they are still quite firm (about 5 minutes). Rinse them in hot water, and set aside to drain on a slightly damp dishcloth.

Melt half the butter in a skillet and cook the spinach and the ham over a low heat for 2 minutes. Remove from the heat, and stir in the mozzarella cheese. Fill each of the cannelloni with the mixture, and put them into a greased ovenproof dish. Melt the remaining butter in a pan, and stir in the flour. Cook for about 1 minute; then take the pan off the heat, and gradually stir in the milk. Bring to a boil, stirring continuously, then cook for 2-3 minutes. Season to taste with nutmeg, salt and pepper. Pour the sauce over the filled cannelloni, and top with Parmesan cheese. Bake for 15 minutes. Serve piping hot.

SPINACH TAGLIATELLE WITH CREAM SAUCE

I sometimes add a little freshly grated nutmeg to this sauce.
The dish is a simple celebration of fragrant flavors.

Serves 4

INGREDIENTS
2¾ cups all-purpose flour
2 eggs
¾ cup cooked and chopped spinach
2 tablespoons freshly chopped chives
Scant 1 cup light cream
Salt and freshly ground black pepper

Mix together the flour, eggs and spinach in a large bowl. Mix well and form the dough into a ball. Knead lightly; then sprinkle the dough with flour, and chill for 30 minutes. Roll out the dough with a rolling pin, or pass it through the rollers of a pasta machine, and then cut it into tagliatelle. Spread the strips out on a floured surface; the strips should not touch one another. Let dry for a few minutes.

Bring a large pan of salted water to a boil. Add the pasta, and cook until *al dente*. Rinse under hot water, and set aside to drain. Heat together the chives and cream. Add the pasta to the pan, and stir well. Serve when the pasta is heated through. Season with a little salt and pepper if necessary.

TAGLIATELLE WITH SAUTÉED VEGETABLES

A delicious recipe for fresh pasta with summer vegetables

Serves 4

INGREDIENTS
2¾ cups all-purpose flour
2 eggs, beaten
2 tablespoons olive oil
1 red bell pepper, seeded and cut into thin strips
2 zucchini, thickly peeled (keep the peel and discard the rest)
Salt and freshly ground black pepper
¼ cup butter

Make the dough by mixing together the flour and eggs. Work the dough with your fingertips, and form into a ball. Set aside to rest in the refrigerator for 30 minutes, wrapped. Pass the dough through the rollers of a pasta machine, flouring the dough lightly to prevent sticking. Alternatively, roll out the dough with a rolling pin. Pass the strips through the pasta machine fitted with a tagliatelle cutter, or cut into strips with a sharp knife. Spread the tagliatelle out on a dishcloth, and let dry for 30 minutes.

Heat the olive oil in a skillet and sauté the pepper for 2 minutes, stirring frequently. Add strips of the zucchini, peel and continue cooking for 45 seconds. Pour off the excess fat, and season with salt and pepper. Keep warm. Cook the tagliatelle in boiling, salted water for about 3 minutes; then rinse under hot water, and let drain. Put the skillet containing the vegetables over the heat. Stir in the butter, and then stir in the tagliatelle. Heat thoroughly, and serve immediately.

NOODLE VEGETABLE RING

An unusual way of serving tagliatelle. Pack the noodles firmly into the mold, so that they will release easily for serving.

Serves 4-6

INGREDIENTS
3 ounces egg noodles or thin
    tagliatelle
Oil
3 tablespoons butter or
    margarine
3 tablespoons all-purpose flour
1½ cups milk
Salt, freshly ground black pepper
    and paprika
2 cups grated Cheddar cheese
2 eggs, beaten
½ cup cooked mixed peas and
    carrots
1 cup cooked broccoli flowerets
1 small red bell pepper, seeded
    and diced

Preheat the oven to 350°F. Cook the egg noodles in boiling, salted water until just tender. Drain well, and toss with a little oil to prevent them from sticking.

Melt the butter or margarine in a saucepan, then stir in the flour. Cook for about 1 minute, then gradually beat in the milk until smooth. Add a good pinch of salt, pepper and paprika. Bring the sauce to a boil, stirring continuously, and cook until thick. Add the cheese, and stir until melted. Divide the sauce in two.

Add half the sauce and the eggs to the noodles, and mix thoroughly. Spoon the mixture into a well-greased ring mold. Put the mold in a roasting pan containing enough hot water to come halfway up the sides of the mold. Bake for about 45 minutes, or until completely set.

Meanwhile, combine the cooked vegetables with the diced bell pepper and the remaining cheese sauce. If the sauce is too thick, add a little more milk. Unmold the noodle ring onto a large platter, and sprinkle with paprika. Spoon the vegetables in their sauce into the center, and serve.

TAGLIATELLE WITH DRIED MUSHROOMS AND CREAM

Dried mushrooms have a very intense flavor. I like to make this dish with a mixture of dried and fresh mushrooms.

Serves 4-6

INGREDIENTS
⅓ cup dried mushrooms or 8 ounces fresh
3 tablespoons olive oil
1 onion, chopped
1 pound tagliatelle
½ cup light cream
¼ cup grated Parmesan cheese
2 tablespoons freshly chopped parsley
Salt and freshly ground black pepper

Soak the dried mushrooms in water for 2-3 hours. Drain and squeeze out the liquid, then chop the mushrooms roughly. Heat the oil in a small pan, and sauté the chopped onion for 1-2 minutes. Add the mushrooms, and cook for an additional 10 minutes. Meanwhile, cook the tagliatelle in plenty of boiling, salted water. Drain and return the pasta to the pan. Stir in the mushrooms, cream, cheese and parsley. Season well with salt and pepper. Stir until heated through and well mixed. Serve at once.

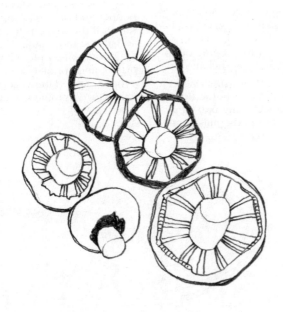

CHINESE NOODLES WITH VEGETABLES

This pasta dish has a taste of the Orient about it. Add fresh mushrooms to the other vegetables in the skillet if Chinese dried mushrooms are not available.

Serves 4

INGREDIENTS
2 tablespoons dried black Chinese mushrooms
2 carrots
¼ cucumber
7-ounce can bamboo shoots
½ cup bean sprouts
14 ounces Chinese noodles
3 tablespoons oil
3 slices fresh gingerroot, peeled
1 clove garlic, finely chopped
1 small chili, finely chopped
5 tablespoons soy sauce
1 tablespoon honey
Salt and freshly ground black pepper
Freshly chopped chives

Soak the mushrooms for 15 minutes in boiling water. Drain; then discard the stalks, and boil the mushroom caps for 5 minutes. Cut the carrots into matchsticks. Squeeze the water from the mushrooms, and slice the caps. Cut the cucumber into chunks. Peel the chunks thickly, and discard the seeds. Cut into matchsticks, then cut the bamboo shoots into matchsticks. Blanch the bamboo shoots for 2 minutes; then drain and set aside. Wash the bean sprouts. Blanch for 1 minute; then plunge into cold water and drain.

Cook the noodles in boiling salted water for a few minutes, the exact cooking time will depend on the thickness of the noodles. Drain, rinse and set aside. Heat the oil in a skillet, and fry the gingerroot, garlic and chilli for a few seconds. Add the bamboo shoots, mushrooms and carrots. Fry for 4 minutes, then add the bean sprouts. Cook for an additional 2 minutes. Add the noodles, soy sauce and honey. Stir well and heat through. Add the cucumber at the last moment. Heat for 1 minute, then season to taste with salt and pepper. Garnish with the chives, and serve.

FIVE-COLORED NOODLES

It's not the pasta that is five-colored, it's the vegetables that are served with it!

Serves 4

INGREDIENTS

4 dried shiitake mushrooms, soaked for 30 minutes, drained and stalks removed, sliced
8 ounces Chinese noodles or thin tagliatelle
⅔ cup chicken stock
1 carrot, cut into diagonal slices
1 small turnip, diced
4 ounces thin green beans, cut into 1½-inch slices
2 teaspoons cornstarch
3 tablespoons light soy sauce
4 teaspoons black sesame seeds

Prepare the dried mushrooms. Cook the noodles in plenty of boiling, salted water for 5 minutes. Drain and rinse under cold water, then drain thoroughly. Bring the stock to a boil in a separate pan, and add the carrot, turnip, mushrooms and beans. Cover and simmer for 8-10 minutes, until just tender. Blend the cornstarch and soy sauce together, and add to the stock. Continue cooking until slightly thickened. Divide the noodles among 4 serving bowls, and add the vegetables. Sprinkle with the black sesame seeds, and serve.

BRAISED NOODLES

I love noodle dishes with plenty of spicy flavors and rich gravy. A large napkin will protect your clothing while you enjoy this dish!

Serves 4

INGREDIENTS
8 ounces Chinese noodles
3 tablespoons oil
6 scallions, chopped
1 small piece fresh gingerroot, grated
1¼ cups chicken or vegetable stock
2 tablespoons soy sauce

Garnish
2 red chilis, seeded and finely chopped
2 tablespoons freshly chopped coriander
½ cup chopped roasted peanuts

Cook the noodles in boiling, salted water until just tender. Drain them, and rinse under hot water. Toss in a colander to remove excess water. Heat the oil in a wok or heavy-bottomed pan, and cook the scallions and gingerroot for about 1 minute. Add the noodles, and fry on one side until golden-brown. Turn over, and fry on the other side until golden. Mix the stock and soy sauce together, and gradually pour over the noodles. Simmer for about 5 minutes, stirring occasionally to help separate the noodles. Serve in individual bowls, sprinkled with the garnish.

STIR-FRIED THAI NOODLES

This is a classic Thai dish. Much of the flavor comes from the pickled turnip, which is not always easy to find, so stock up whenever you are near a specialty food store.

Serves 4

INGREDIENTS

6 ounces rice noodles
4 tablespoons oil
8 ounces tofu, cut into cubes
3 cloves garlic, crushed
½ cup dried shrimp
3 tablespoons chopped pickled turnip
4 tablespoons fish sauce
2 tablespoons palm sugar
1 tablespoon soy sauce
2 tablespoons tamarind juice
2 eggs, beaten
1 tablespoon freshly chopped garlic chives
½ cup chopped roasted peanuts
8 ounces bean sprouts
Chili strips, to garnish

Soak the rice noodles in boiling water for 10-15 minutes, or until softened; then drain and set aside.

Heat the oil in a wok or heavy-bottomed pan, and fry the tofu cubes until browned on all sides. Remove with a draining spoon, and set aside. Add the garlic and dried shrimp to the wok or pan, and stir-fry for 2 minutes. Reduce the heat, and add the noodles. Cook for 5 minutes, tossing the ingredients frequently. Add the pickled turnip, fish sauce, palm sugar, soy sauce and tamarind juice, and cook for 2 minutes. Add the beaten egg, and cook, tossing the ingredients together, until the egg sets. Stir in the tofu, garlic chives, peanuts and bean sprouts. Garnish with chili strips, and serve immediately.

PASTA AND VEGETABLES IN PARMESAN DRESSING

There is one problem with this recipe – the dressing is so delicious that I tend to eat it by itself!

Serves 6

INGREDIENTS

1 pound pasta spirals or other shapes
8 ounces assorted vegetables such as:
Zucchini, cut in slices or matchsticks
Broccoli, trimmed into very small florets
Snow peas, trimmed
Carrots, cut in slices or matchsticks
Celery, cut in matchsticks
Scallions, thinly shredded or sliced
Asparagus tips
Green beans, sliced
Red or yellow bell peppers, seeded and thinly sliced
Cucumber, cut in matchsticks

Dressing
⅔ cup olive oil
3 tablespoons lemon juice
1 tablespoon pepper sauce
1 tablespoon freshly chopped parsley
1 tablespoon freshly chopped basil
½ cup grated Parmesan cheese
2 tablespoons mild mustard
Salt and freshly ground black pepper
Pinch of sugar

Cook the pasta in a large pan of boiling, salted water for 10-12 minutes, or until just tender. Rinse under hot water, then leave in cold water. Cook all the vegetables except the cucumber in boiling, salted water for 3 minutes until just tender. Rinse in cold water, and let drain. Mix the dressing ingredients together. Drain the pasta thoroughly, and toss it with the dressing. Add the vegetables, and toss until coated. Chill for up to 1 hour before serving.

TAGLIATELLE WITH SUMMER SAUCE

This recipe is slightly unusual as a cold sauce is added to hot pasta – but it works well.

Serves 4

INGREDIENTS

Pasta Dough
1 cup all-purpose flour
⅔ cup fine semolina
2 large eggs, lightly beaten
2 teaspoons olive oil

Sauce
1 pound unpeeled tomatoes, seeded and chopped
1 large green bell pepper, seeded and diced
1 onion, chopped
1 tablespoon freshly chopped basil
1 tablespoon freshly chopped parsley
2 cloves garlic, crushed
⅔ cup olive oil and vegetable oil, mixed

Put the flour and semolina into a bowl, and make a well in the center. Put the eggs and oil in the well, and mix to a dough, using a fork and then your hand. Knead the dough until smooth, then cover the dough and let it rest for 15 minutes. Divide the dough into quarters, and roll it out thinly with a rolling pin on a floured surface, or use a pasta machine, dusting the dough lightly with flour before rolling. Let the sheets of pasta dry for about 10 minutes on a floured surface or dishcloths. Cut the sheets into strips about ¼ inch wide by hand or machine, dusting lightly with flour while cutting. Let the cut pasta dry while preparing the sauce.

Combine all the sauce ingredients, mixing well. The flavor will develop if the sauce can be left to marinate. Cook the pasta for 5-6 minutes in boiling, salted water. Drain the pasta, and rinse under very hot water. Toss in a colander to drain excess water. Put the hot pasta into serving dish. Pour the cold sauce over and toss. Serve immediately.

SPAGHETTI AMATRICIANA

*This is a dish of spaghetti with a spicy tomato sauce. Serve
with grated Parmesan, if required.*

Serves 4

INGREDIENTS
1 onion
6 rindless slices smoked bacon
1 pound ripe tomatoes
1 red chili
1½ tablespoons oil
12 ounces spaghetti

Slice the onion thinly. Cut the bacon into thin strips. Scald the tomatoes in boiling water for 6-8 seconds. Remove with a draining spoon, and put into cold water. Let cool completely. Skin the tomatoes, and cut them in half; then remove the seeds and pulp with a teaspoon. Press the seeds and pulp through a strainer, and retain the juice to use in the sauce if wished. Chop the tomato flesh roughly, and set it aside. Cut the stem off the chili, and cut it in half lengthwise.

Remove the seeds and core, and cut the chili into thin strips. Cut the strips into small dice.

Heat the oil in a sauté or skillet, and add the onion and bacon. Stir over a medium heat for about 5 minutes, until the onion is transparent. Drain off any excess fat. Add the tomatoes and chili, and mix well. Simmer the sauce slowly, uncovered, for about 5 minutes, stirring occasionally. Meanwhile, cook the spaghetti in boiling, salted water for about 10-12 minutes. Drain and rinse in hot water; then toss in a colander to dry. To serve, spoon the sauce on top of the spaghetti.

LASAGNE NAPOLETANA

Lasagne as eaten in Naples – with a tomato sauce. Ideal for vegetarians.

Serves 6

INGREDIENTS
9 sheets spinach lasagne

Tomato Sauce
3 tablespoons olive oil
2 cloves garlic, crushed
2 pounds fresh tomatoes, skinned, or canned tomatoes, drained
2 tablespoons freshly chopped basil, six whole leaves reserved
Salt and freshly ground black pepper
Pinch of sugar

Cheese Filling
1 pound ricotta cheese
¼ cup unsalted butter
2 cups grated mozzarella cheese
Salt and freshly ground black pepper
Pinch of nutmeg

Preheat the oven to 375°F. Cook the pasta for 8 minutes in boiling, salted water. Drain and rinse under hot water; then spread out in a single layer on a damp dishcloth until required.

To prepare the sauce, cook the garlic in the oil for about 1 minute in a large pan. When pale brown, add the tomatoes, basil, salt, pepper and sugar. If using fresh tomatoes, drop into boiling water for 6-8 seconds. Transfer to cold water, and let cool completely before removing the skins. This will make the skins easier to remove. Simmer the sauce for 35 minutes. Add more seasoning or sugar to taste. Beat the ricotta cheese and butter for the filling together until creamy, then stir in the remaining ingredients.

To assemble the lasagne, oil a rectangular ovenproof dish, and lay 3 sheets of lasagne in the bottom. Cover with one-third of the sauce, and carefully add a layer of cheese. Lay another 3 sheets of pasta over the cheese, and cover with another third of the sauce. Add the remaining cheese filling, and cover with the remaining pasta. Spoon the remaining sauce on top. Cover with foil, and bake for 20 minutes. Uncover the dish, and cook for an additional 10 minutes. Garnish with the reserved basil leaves before serving.

SPIRALI WITH SPINACH AND BACON

A quick and tasty dish to prepare – I often add freshly grated nutmeg, the perfect partner for spinach.

Serves 4

INGREDIENTS

12 ounces pasta spirals
8 ounces fresh spinach
4 bacon slices
1 small chili, red or green
1 small red bell pepper
1 small onion
3 tablespoons olive oil
1 clove garlic, crushed
Salt and freshly ground black
  pepper

Cook the pasta in boiling, salted water for about 10-12 minutes, or until just tender. Drain in a colander, and rinse under hot water. Keep the pasta in a bowl of hot water until ready to use.

Tear the stalks off the spinach, and wash the leaves well, changing the water several times. Set aside to drain. Remove any rind and bones from the bacon, and dice the bacon finely. Cut the chili and red bell pepper in half; remove the seeds, and slice finely. Slice the onion thinly. Roll up several of the spinach leaves together into a cigar shape, and then shred them finely. Repeat until all the spinach is shredded.

Heat the oil in a sauté or skillet, and add the garlic, onion, chili, bell pepper and bacon. Fry for 2 minutes; then add the spinach, and fry for an additional 2 minutes, stirring continuously. Season with salt and pepper. Drain the pasta, and toss it in a colander to remove excess water. Mix with the spinach sauce, and serve immediately.

NOODLES WITH GINGER AND OYSTER SAUCE

This makes a very good accompaniment to any Chinese meat or chicken dishes, but is also a tasty snack on its own.

Serves 4 or 2 as a snack

INGREDIENTS
8 ounces Chinese noodles
1 carrot
1 zucchini
3 slices of fresh gingerroot, peeled
1 tablespoon oil
1 scallion, finely sliced
1 tablespoon soy sauce
2 tablespoons oyster sauce
Salt and freshly ground black pepper

Cook the noodles in boiling, salted water as directed on the package. Rinse them under cold water, and set aside to drain. Cut the carrot into thin strips. Thickly peel the zucchini to include a little of the flesh, and cut the peel into thin strips. Discard the center of the zucchini. Peel the fresh gingerroot sparingly, but remove any hard parts. Cut into thin slices, using a potato peeler. Cut the slices into thin strips, using a very sharp knife. Heat the oil in a wok or heavy-bottomed skillet, and stir-fry the scallion for 10 seconds. Add the carrot, zucchini and gingerroot, and stir-fry briefly. Stir in the noodles, and cook for 1 minute. Stir in the soy and oyster sauces, and continue cooking until heated through. Season with salt and pepper, and serve.

SPICY FRIED NOODLES

This recipe may be made with thread egg noodles or the thin, flat mie noodles, which are like fine tagliatelle. I actually prefer to use the latter.

Serves 4

INGREDIENTS
8 ounces Chinese noodles
3 tablespoons oil
1 onion, finely chopped
2 cloves garlic, crushed
1 small piece fresh gingerroot, grated
½ teaspoon ground cumin
½ teaspoon ground coriander
¼ teaspoon ground nutmeg
¼ teaspoon ground cinnamon
¼ teaspoon cayenne pepper
Salt and pepper
6 tablespoons soy sauce

Garnish
Thin omelet strips
1 stalk celery, very thinly shredded

Cook the noodles in boiling, salted water until just tender. Drain and refresh under hot water, tossing in a colander to remove excess water. Heat the oil in a large, heavy-bottomed skillet or wok, and fry the onion, garlic and gingerroot until softened. Add the spices, and cook for an additional 2 minutes. Stir in the noodles, and then fry over a low heat for about 3 minutes. Add the soy sauce, and season with salt and pepper. Serve topped with the garnishes.

TOFU WITH CRISPY NOODLES

Fried noodles give a wonderful crispy texture to this unusual dish.

Serves 4

INGREDIENTS
Oil for deep-frying
4 ounces rice noodles
  (vermicelli)
8 ounces tofu, drained and
  patted dry
2 carrots, peeled and sliced
¾ broccoli flowerets
2 stalks celery, sliced
1 onion, cut into wedges
1 teaspoon shrimp paste
2 tablespoons light soy sauce
3 tablespoons white wine vinegar
2 tablespoons dark muscovado
  sugar
1 teaspoon grated fresh
  gingerroot

Heat the oil to 360°F in a wok or heavy-bottomrd skillet. Add the rice noodles in small batches; turn over, and fry for a few seconds. The noodles will puff up immediately. Remove from the oil, and drain well on paper towels.

Cut the tofu into cubes, and fry for a few minutes until browned on all sides; remove from the oil, and set aside.

Pour off most of the oil. Add the carrots, broccoli, celery and onion to the wok or pan, and stir-fry for 2 minutes, or until the vegetables are cooked but still crisp. Stir in the shrimp paste, soy sauce, vinegar, sugar and gingerroot. Return the vermicelli and tofu to the wok or pan. Toss to mix, and serve immediately.

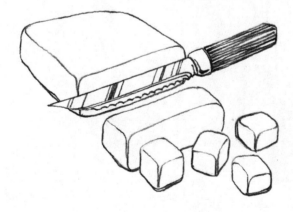

NOODLES WITH PEPPERS AND GINGER

*This is a very fragrant way of cooking noodles. Cutting the
bell peppers so finely releases plenty of flavor from
the vegetables.*

Serves 4

INGREDIENTS
1 red bellpepper, seeded
1 green bell pepper, seeded
8 ounces Chinese noodles
1 tablespoon oil
1 teaspoon chopped fresh
  gingerroot
Salt and freshly ground black
  pepper
1 clove garlic, finely chopped

Cut the bell peppers into six
pieces. Cut each of these pieces
in half through the flesh of the
bell pepper, to form wide, thin
slices. Cut each slice into very
thin matchsticks. Cook the
noodles until just tender in
boiling, lightly salted water,
stirring occasionally so that they
do not stick. Drain the noodles in
a strainer, and rinse under cold
running water. Set aside to drain.
Heat the oil in a wok or heavy-
bottomed skillet, and stir-fry the
bell peppers, gingerroot and
garlic for 1 minute, stirring
continuously. Add the well-
drained noodles, and stir-fry until
the noodles are hot. Season to
taste, and serve immediately.

PASTA AND ASPARAGUS SALAD

I can never decide whether green or egg pasta looks best in this elegant, summer salad.

Serves 4

Ingredients

4 ounces tagliatelle or other pasta shapes
1 pound asparagus, trimmed and cut into 1-inch pieces
2 zucchini, cut into 2-inch sticks
2 tablespoons freshly chopped parsley
2 tablespoons freshly chopped marjoram
1 lemon, peeled and segmented
Grated peel and juice of 1 lemon
6 tablespoons olive oil
Pinch of unrefined sugar
Salt and freshly ground black pepper
Crisp lettuce leaves
Curly chicory leaves

Cook the pasta in plenty of boiling, salted water for 10 minutes, or as directed on the package. Drain and refresh in cold water. Drain again, and let cool completely. Cook the asparagus in lightly salted, boiling water for 4 minutes; then add the zucchini, and cook for an additional 3-4 minutes, or until the vegetables are just tender. Drain and refresh in cold water. Drain again and let cool.

Put the cooked pasta, vegetables, herbs and lemon segments into a large bowl, taking care not to break up the vegetables. Mix together the lemon peel, juice, oil, sugar, salt and pepper to make the dressing. Arrange the lettuce and chicory leaves on serving plates. Just before serving, pour the dressing over the vegetables and pasta, and toss to coat well. Pile equal quantities of the pasta salad into the center of the salad leaves, and serve immediately.

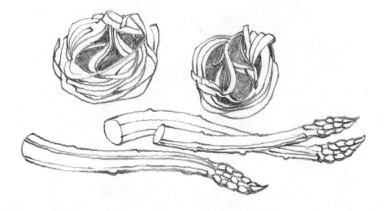

89

PASTA, PEAS AND BELL PEPPERS

This colorful lunch dish is also an excellent salad to serve as part of a buffet.

Serves 4

INGREDIENTS

8 ounces mixed, plain and whole wheat, pasta shells
Salt
1½ cups shelled peas
1 green bell pepper, seeded and sliced
1 red bell pepper, seeded and sliced
1 yellow bell pepper, seeded and sliced
⅔ cup vegetable or olive oil
4 tablespoons white wine vinegar
1 tablespoon Dijon or wholegrain mustard
2 teaspoons poppy seeds
2 teaspoons freshly chopped parsley
1 teaspoon freshly chopped thyme
Freshly ground black pepper
4 scallion, trimmed and shredded
1 cup finely grated Cheddar cheese

Cook the pasta in plenty of boiling, salted water for 10 minutes, or as directed on the package. Drain the pasta, and cool under running water. When cold, drain well. Cook the peas and bell peppers in boiling water for 5 minutes. Drain and add to the pasta.

Put the oil, vinegar, mustard, poppy seeds, herbs and a little seasoning into a bowl, and whisk vigorously until the dressing is thick and pale in color. Pour the dressing over the pasta. Toss well, and chill until required. Stir the scallions and cheese into the salad just before serving.

PASTA PRIMAVERA

A classic dish of pasta and young spring vegetables. The flavors should be intense.

Serves 4

INGREDIENTS
1 pound pasta of your choice
Salt
8 ounces asparagus
4 ounces green beans, trimmed
2 carrots, sliced
¼ cup butter
⅔ cup sliced mushrooms
Freshly ground black pepper
3 tomatoes, peeled, seeded and
  chopped
6 scallions, trimmed and sliced
⅔ cup heavy cream
2 tablespoons freshly chopped
  parsley
2 tablespoons freshly chopped
  tarragon

Cook the pasta in plenty of boiling, salted water for 10 minutes, or as directed on the package. Meanwhile, trim any woody ends from the asparagus, and cut each stalk diagonally into 1-inch pieces, leaving the tips whole. Blanch the asparagus, beans and carrots for 3 minutes in boiling water, then drain well.

Melt the butter in a large pan. Add the blanched vegetables and mushrooms, then sauté for 3 minutes. Stir in the tomatoes and scallions, then add the cream, seasonings and herbs, and bring to a boil. Boil rapidly for a few minutes until the cream thickens slightly. When the pasta is cooked, drain well, and add it to the pan. Toss to combine all the ingredients, and serve immediately.

PASTA-STUFFED CABBAGE LEAVES

Use a small pasta for the stuffing, or the cabbage leaves will not roll up easily around the mixture.

Serves 4

4 ounces small pasta shapes for soup
Salt
8-12 large cabbage leaves, washed
1 hard-cooked egg, finely chopped
½ cup chopped walnuts
1 tablespoon freshly chopped chives
2 tablespoons freshly chopped parsley
1 teaspoon freshly chopped marjoram
Freshly ground black pepper
1¼ cups vegetable stock
1 tablespoon walnut oil
1 onion, finely chopped
1 green bell pepper, seeded and chopped
15-ounce can chopped tomatoes
1⅓ cups chopped button mushrooms
2 tablespoons tomato paste
1 bay leaf
Pinch of unrefined sugar

Preheat the oven to 350°F. Cook the pasta in plenty of boiling, salted water for 8 minutes, or as directed on the package. Remove the thick stem from the base of the cabbage leaves. Blanch the leaves in boiling water for 3 minutes; then drain and refresh them in cold water. When the pasta is cooked, drain it well. Mix with the egg, walnuts and herbs, then season lightly. Divide the pasta mixture between the cabbage leaves. Fold up to enclose the filling completely, and secure with tooth picks. Put the cabbage rolls into a shallow ovenproof dish, and add the stock. Cover the dish, and bake for 40 minutes.

Heat the oil in a skillet, and fry the onion and bell pepper for 5 minutes, or until soft. Stir in the tomatoes, mushrooms, tomato paste, bay leaf and sugar. Season to taste, and cook slowly for 10 minutes. Remove the cabbage packages from the dish with a draining spoon, and serve with the sauce poured over them.

TRICOLORED TAGLIATELLE AND VEGETABLES

This lunch dish is subtly flavored with garlic and rosemary.

Serves 4

INGREDIENTS

8 ounces tricolored tagliatelle
(mixture of tomato, spinach
and egg pasta)
Salt
¼ cup butter or margarine
1 large onion, sliced
8 ounces broccoli flowerets
2 red bell peppers, seeded and
sliced
2 cloves garlic, crushed
2 teaspoons freshly chopped
rosemary
¾ cup finely grated Cheddar
cheese
Freshly ground black pepper

Cook the pasta in plenty of boiling, salted water for 10 minutes, or as directed on the package. Meanwhile, melt half the butter in a skillet, and sauté the onion for 4 minutes; then add the broccoli and bell peppers, and cook for an additional 5 minutes, or until all the vegetables are tender.

In a separate pan, heat the garlic, rosemary and the remaining butter slowly for a few minutes until the butter melts and the flavors combine. When the pasta is cooked, drain well and return to the pan. Drain the garlic mixture through a strainer onto the pasta – this gives a very subtle hint of garlic and rosemary to the pasta. Add the cooked vegetables and cheese. Season to taste, and toss well before serving.

MEATLESS SPAGHETTI BOLOGNESE

I particularly like the flavor of aduki beans, but any cooked beans could be used in this dish.

Serves 2-4

INGREDIENTS

12 ounces whole wheat spaghetti
4 tablespoons olive oil
8 ounces onions, chopped
1 clove garlic, crushed
15-ounce can tomatoes, chopped and juice retained
1 cup diced carrots
2 stalks celery, sliced
1⅓ cups sliced mushrooms
1 small red bell pepper, seeded and diced
1 tablespoon freshly chopped basil
1 tablespoon freshly chopped oregano
¼ teaspoon nutmeg
2 tablespoons tomato paste
1¼ cups stock or water
1 cup cooked aduki beans
2 teaspoons soya flour or cornstarch
Salt and freshly ground black pepper
Grated Parmesan cheese

Cook the spaghetti in plenty of boiling, salted water until just tender, or as directed on the package.

Heat the olive oil in a large pan, and cook the onions and garlic until browned. Add the canned tomatoes with their juice, the carrots, celery, mushrooms, bell pepper, basil, oregano, nutmeg, tomato paste, and stock. Stir well, and simmer for about 20 minutes, or until the vegetables are cooked. Add the cooked beans, and heat for an additional 5 minutes.

Mix the soya flour with a little water, and add it to the sauce. Cook for 2 minutes, until boiling and slightly thickened. Season to taste. Drain the spaghetti, and serve, topped with the sauce and a sprinkling of Parmesan cheese.

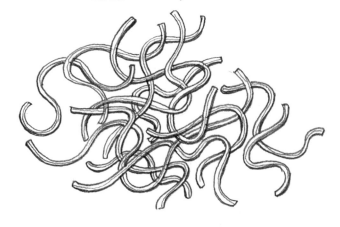

RATATOUILLE LASAGNE

A combination of two favorite dishes – the warmth and brightness of ratatouille and the comfort of a baked lasagne.

Serves 4-6

INGREDIENTS

6 strips green or whole wheat lasagne
2-3 tablespoons olive oil
2 onions, finely chopped
2 cloves garlic, crushed
1 large eggplant, chopped
1 zucchini, thinly sliced
1 green bell pepper, seeded and chopped
1 red bell pepper, seeded and chopped
14-ounce can chopped tomatoes
2-3 tablespoons tomato paste
A little vegetable stock
Salt and freshly ground black pepper

White sauce
2 tablespoons butter or margarine
¼ cup whole wheat flour
1¼ cups milk

⅓ cup grated Parmesan cheese
Freshly chopped parsley, to garnish

Preheat the oven to 350°F. Cook the lasagne in boiling, salted water for 12-15 minutes, then rinse it in cold water to prevent overcooking or sticking.

Heat the oil in a pan, and fry the onion and garlic until soft. Add the eggplant, zucchini and bell peppers, and cook until soft. Add the tomatoes with their juice and the tomato paste, and simmer until the vegetables are tender. It may be necessary to add a little stock at this stage. Season well, and set aside until required. Make the white sauce by melting the butter or margarine in a small pan. Add the flour, and cook for 1 minute; then gradually add the milk, stirring continuously. Bring to a boil, and simmer for about 5 minutes. Remove the pan from the heat.

Grease a deep ovenproof dish, and layer the ratatouille and lasagne in it, starting with the ratatouille and finishing with a layer of lasagne. Pour the white sauce over the lasagne, and top with the Parmesan cheese. Bake for 35 minutes until golden. Garnish with parsley before serving.

ZUCCHINI AND CORN BAKE

A simple but delicious vegetarian pasta bake, and a good way of using up leftover pasta.

Serves 4

INGREDIENTS
1 tablespoon oil
1 onion, chopped
8 ounces zucchini, sliced
7-ounce can corn, drained
6 ounces pasta shapes, cooked
Large pinch of dried oregano
1 tablespoon tomato paste
Salt and freshly ground black
  pepper

Sauce
2 tablespoons butter or
  margarine
¼ cup whole wheat flour
1¼ cups milk
3 tablespoons white wine
½ cup grated sharp cheese

Topping
½ cup whole wheat bread
  crumbs
1 tablespoon sunflower seeds

Preheat the oven to 350°F. Heat the oil in a skillet, and cook the chopped onion until soft. Add the sliced zucchini and brown lightly; then mix in the corn, cooked pasta, oregano and tomato paste, and stir. Season lightly, and transfer the mixture to a greased ovenproof dish.

Make the cheese sauce by melting the butter or margarine and stirring in the flour. Cook slowly for a few seconds, and then gradually add the milk and wine, stirring continuously, to make a smooth sauce. Bring to a boil, stirring continuously. Add the grated cheese, and stir until it melts into the sauce. Remove the pan from the heat, and pour the sauce over the vegetable mixture. Top with the bread crumbs and sunflower seeds. Bake for about 20 minutes until browned and bubbling.

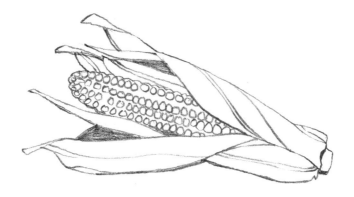

PASTA AND AVOCADO SALAD

A tasty combination of wholesome ingredients producing a filling salad.

Serves 4

INGREDIENTS
8 ounces pasta shapes
3 tablespoons mayonnaise
1 tablespoon tahini
1 orange
½ red bell pepper, seeded and chopped
1 avocado
Pumpkin seeds, to garnish

Cook the pasta in plenty of boiling, salted water until soft; then drain, and let cool. Mix together the mayonnaise and tahini. Segment the orange, and chop it into small pieces, retaining any juice. Chop the bell pepper.

Stir the mayonnaise mixture, bell pepper and orange (plus juice) into the pasta. Just before serving, dice the avocado, and carefully stir it into the salad. Serve on an oval platter, garnished with pumpkin seeds.

CONCHIGLIE WITH TWO SAUCES

The tomato and mushroom sauces offer a contrast of colors and textures within one dish.

Serves 4

INGREDIENTS
1 pound conchiglie (pasta shells), cooked

Tomato sauce
1 large onion, very finely chopped
1 teaspoon stock powder or half a bouillon cube
3 tablespoons water
1 clove garlic, crushed
½ teaspoon dried thyme
Pinch ground rosemary
14-ounce can tomatoes

Mushroom sauce
9 ounces oyster mushrooms
2 tablespoons butter or margarine
1 teaspoon stock powder or half a bouillon cube
4 tablespoons fromage frais
Freshly chopped parsley to garnish

To make the tomato sauce, put the onion, stock powder, water and garlic into a pan, and cook very slowly for 7-10 minutes, until the onion is soft. Add the thyme and rosemary, and cook for 1 minute. Chop the canned tomatoes, and add them to the pan with the tomato juice. Bring to a boil, and boil rapidly until the sauce has reduced and thickened.

To make the mushroom sauce, chop the mushrooms finely. Melt the butter or margarine in a pan, and add the stock powder or a bouillon cube and mushrooms. Simmer very gently for 10-15 minutes; then remove the pan from the heat, and stir in the fromage frais. Heat slowly until hot, but do not boil.

Divide the pasta between 4 plates, and pour the tomato sauce over one half of the pasta and the mushroom sauce over the other half. Sprinkle the chopped parsley between the two sauces, and serve at once.

SPICY ORIENTAL NOODLES

This is a complete meal in itself, but is also delicious with sliced cold meat or chicken.

Serves 4

INGREDIENTS

8 ounces Chinese noodles (medium thickness)
5 tablespoons oil
4 carrots
8 ounces broccoli
12 Chinese dried mushrooms, soaked for 30 minutes
4 scallions, sliced diagonally
1 clove garlic
1-2 teaspoons chili sauce, mild or hot
4 tablespoons soy sauce
4 tablespoons rice wine or dry sherry
2 teaspoons cornstarch

Cook the noodles in boiling salted water for about 4-5 minutes. Drain well; then rinse under hot water to remove the excess starch, and drain again. Toss with about 1 tablespoon of the oil to prevent sticking. Using a large, sharp knife, slice the carrots thinly on the diagonal. Cut the flowerets off the broccoli, and divide into equal but not too small sections. Slice the stalks thinly on the diagonal. If they seem tough, peel them before slicing. Blanch the vegetables in boiling water for about 2 minutes; then drain and rinse under cold water to stop further cooking. Let drain. Remove and discard the mushroom stems, and slice the caps thinly. Set aside with the onions.

Heat a wok or heavy-bottomed skillet, and add the remaining oil with the garlic clove. Leave the garlic in the pan while the oil heats, and then remove and discard it. Add the carrots and broccoli, and stir-fry for about 1 minute. Add the mushrooms and onions, and continue to stir-fry, tossing the vegetables in the pan continuously. Combine the chili sauce, soy sauce, wine and cornstarch, mixing well. Pour the mixture over the vegetables, and cook until the sauce boils and clears. Toss with the noodles, and heat through. Serve immediately.

CAPONATA AND NOODLES

Caponata is a Sicilian dish of eggplants in a well-flavored tomato sauce. This recipe is for a quick caponata mixed with noodles.

Serves 4

INGREDIENTS

1 onion, thinly sliced
2 tablespoons olive oil
2 cloves garlic, finely chopped
1 large green bell pepper, seeded and diced
1 large red bell pepper, seeded and diced
1 eggplant, diced
6 tomatoes, peeled, seeded and chopped
1 tablespoon tomato paste
3 tablespoons red wine
Salt and freshly ground black pepper
4 ounces green noodles, cooked
¾ cup grated cheese, Parmesan, Cheddar or a mixture of both

Fry the onion slowly in the olive oil for 4 minutes. Add the garlic, red and green bell peppers, eggplant and chopped tomatoes, and cook, covered, for an additional 5 minutes. Add the tomato paste, wine, and salt and pepper to taste, then simmer slowly for 10-15 minutes, until the vegetables are almost soft. Remove from the heat, and stir in the cooked noodles. Spoon into a shallow flameproof dish, and scatter with the grated cheese. Brown under a preheated broiler before serving.

TAGLIATELLE WITH RICH TOMATO SAUCE

This is my favorite tomato sauce recipe – it is rich, packed with flavor and satisfying.

Serves 3-4

INGREDIENTS

12 ounces tagliatelle
3 tablespoons olive oil
2 tablespoons butter
1 large onion, finely sliced
2¼ cups passata (strained tomato purée)
2 eggs, beaten
¼ cup freshly grated Parmesan cheese
6 leaves fresh basil, torn into small pieces
Salt and freshly ground black pepper

Cook the tagliatelle in plenty of boiling, salted water until just tender but still firm. Meanwhile, heat the oil with the butter. Add the onion, and cook until soft. Stir in the passata. Bring to a boil, and cook for 5 minutes, until slightly thickened. Let the sauce cool very slightly, then stir in the eggs, mixing thoroughly and cooking very gently until they thicken the mixture. Add half the Parmesan and the basil. Season with salt and pepper.

Drain the pasta, and rinse in boiling water. Drain again, and return it to the pan. Add half the sauce, and mix well. Serve the remaining sauce over the pasta with the rest of the Parmesan cheese.

ZUCCHINI SPAGHETTI

This dish is simplicity itself – cook the zucchini until soft so that they blend well with the pasta.

Serves 4

INGREDIENTS
12 ounces spaghetti
4 tablespoons olive oil
¼ cup butter
4 zucchini, trimmed and sliced
Salt and freshly ground black
  pepper
⅓ cup freshly grated Parmesan
  cheese

Cook the spaghetti in plenty of boiling, salted water until just tender but still firm. While the spaghetti is cooking, heat the oil and butter together in a large skillet, and cook the zucchini until soft. Drain the pasta; rinse in boiling water, then drain again. Return the pasta to the pan. Add the zucchini and all their cooking juices, and some salt and pepper, and toss together well. Serve with the freshly grated Parmesan cheese.

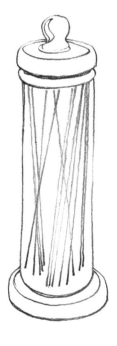

TAGLIATELLE WITH GARLIC AND OIL

This is such a simple recipe but very delicious. I usually serve it as a lunch dish with a salad, but it could also be used to accompany a casserole.

Serves 2

INGREDIENTS

10 ounces green tagliatelle
⅔ pint olive oil
3 cloves garlic, crushed
2 tablespoons freshly chopped parsley
Salt and freshly ground black pepper

Cook the tagliatelle in lots of boiling, salted water for 10 minutes, or until tender but still firm. Stir occasionally. Meanwhile, make the sauce. Heat the oil in a pan, and, when warm, add the garlic. Fry slowly until golden-brown, then add the chopped parsley, and salt and pepper to taste. Drain the tagliatelle. Add the sauce, and toss to coat the pasta well. Serve hot.

NOODLES IN CURRY SAUCE

This makes an excellent lunch dish – warming and tasty but not too heavy.

Serves 4

INGREDIENTS

1 pound thin egg noodles
2 tablespoons butter or
  margarine
1 onion, finely chopped
1 clove garlic, crushed
2 teaspoons ground coriander
1 teaspoon ground fenugreek
1 teaspoon ground cumin
1 teaspoon ground turmeric
Pinch of cayenne pepper
1-2 bananas, peeled and sliced
Juice of ½ lime
1¼ cups stock
1¼ cups whole milk yogurt
2 teaspoons freshly chopped
  mint
Salt and freshly ground black
  pepper

Cook the noodles in boiling salted water until tender. Rinse under hot water, and let drain. Melt the butter or margarine in a large pan, and cook the onion until soft. Add the garlic and spices. Cook for 1 minute, then add the bananas and lime juice. Cook to soften the bananas slightly, mashing them with a fork. Add the stock. Cover the pan, and cook for 20 minutes. Purée in a blender or food processor. Return the sauce to the rinsed-out pan, and bring back to a boil. Remove from the heat, and add the yogurt, mint, and salt and pepper. Pour the sauce over the noodles, and toss before serving.

PASTA SPIRALS WITH CREAMY PARSLEY SAUCE

A light lunch dish, as delicious by itself as with chicken or fish.

Serves 4

INGREDIENTS
2 tablespoons butter or margarine
2 tablespoons all-purpose flour
1¼ cups milk
10 ounces pasta spirals
1 tablespoon lemon juice, or 2 teaspoons wine vinegar
1 tablespoon freshly chopped parsley
Salt and freshly ground black pepper

Melt the butter in a saucepan, then stir in flour. Cook for 1 minute. Remove the pan from the heat, and gradually stir in the milk. Return the pan to the heat, and stir continuously until boiling. Cook for 2 minutes.

Meanwhile, cook the pasta spirals in plenty of boiling, salted water for 10 minutes, or until tender but still firm. Rinse in hot water, and drain well. Add the lemon juice and parsley to the sauce, and stir well. Season if necessary. Pour the sauce over the pasta, and mix well. Serve immediately.

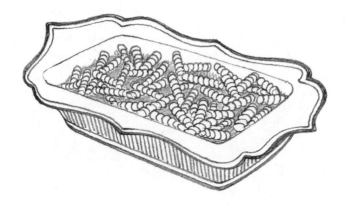

KREPLACH

Kreplach are Jewish ravioli or filled dumplings. They are very similar to Italian ravioli or Chinese wontons. Different fillings are traditionally used at different feasts.

Makes about 50

INGREDIENTS

Kreplach dough
2 cups all-purpose flour
½ teaspoon salt
2 eggs, lightly beaten
2 tablespoons cold water
Additional all-purpose flour for
  dusting

Potato and Mushroom Filling
10 potatoes, boiled in their skins
2 tablespoons butter
2 onions, finely chopped
½ cup dried mushrooms, soaked
  in warm water for 10 minutes
½ teaspoon salt
½ teaspoon black pepper

To make the dough, sift the flour and salt into a bowl. Make a well in the center, and add the eggs and water. Gradually incorporate the flour into the eggs until you have a stiff dough. Cover the bowl, and let the dough rest while you prepare the filling.

Peel and mash the potatoes. Melt the butter in a skillet over a high heat, and sauté the onions until lightly browned. Set aside. Drain the mushrooms, and briefly sauté them in the remaining butter. Mix the mashed potatoes, sautéed onions and sautéed mushrooms, then season the mixture with salt and pepper.

When ready to fill, roll out the dough until ¹⁄₁₆ inch thick on a lightly floured counter. Use a ravioli cutter or sharp knife to cut the dough into 2-inch squares. Put a heaped teaspoonful of the filling in the center of each square. Fold the dough over the filling to form a triangle. Wet your fingers, and pinch the edges of the dough firmly together to prevent the filling from escaping. To cook filled kreplach, drop them into boiling, salted water, and cook for 15 minutes. Drain well before serving.

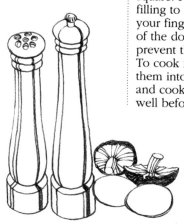

NOODLE KUGEL

These baked noodles are a traditional Jewish accompaniment to a Sabbath stew. They are cooked for a very long time, and become light and fragrant. Keep the dish very tightly covered to prevent the noodles from drying out.

Serves 8

INGREDIENTS
½ cup bread crumbs
8 ounces noodles, cooked and
 drained
¾ cup chicken fat or butter
½ teaspoon salt
½ teaspoon black pepper
2 eggs, lightly beaten

Preheat the oven to 450°F. Grease a large casserole or baking dish, and sprinkle with the bread crumbs. Combine the remaining ingredients in a large bowl, and pour into the prepared dish. Cover tightly with foil. Bake for 30 minutes, then reduce the temperature to 375°F, and bake for an additional 30 minutes. Reduce the temperature again to about 200°F, and cook for at least 4 more hours. Serve with stew or other meats.

MACARONI WITH OLIVE SAUCE

Make this dish with green or black olives, or a mixture of both. It is pungent and delicious. I garnish it with chopped anchovies.

Serves 4

INGREDIENTS
12 ounces macaroni
¼ cup butter
1 clove garlic, finely chopped
10 olives, pitted and finely chopped
Salt and freshly ground black pepper

Cook the macaroni in boiling, salted water until tender but still firm. Rinse in hot water, and set aside to drain. Melt the butter in a saucepan, and add the garlic and olives. Cook for 1 minute, and then stir in the macaroni. Check the seasoning, adding salt and pepper as necessary. Serve hot.

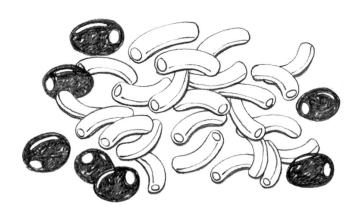

PASTA WITH NUTS, BEANS & CHEESE

There are so many delicious ways of serving pasta with nuts, beans or cheese. Wonderful recipes can be made from a selection of ingredients suitable for most vegetarians, and anyone who does not eat meat need never find their food limited or boring if they are inventive with pasta. I often judge a restaurant by the creativity of their vegetarian pasta dishes, despite the fact that I am a meat-eater myself.

Pine Nuts for Pasta

The first time that I appeared on television, the presenter asked me where pine nuts come from and I was absolutely floored! My answer – out of a package! The small, pale nuts, which are technically kernels, are from the stone pine. They have a high oil content, and do not keep well, becoming rancid, especially in hot weather, so it is advisable to buy them in small quantities and to use them quickly. That said, they have a most wonderful flavor and a delightful texture. I sometimes toast them in a dry skillet before adding to cooked pasta as this releases even more of their delicate flavor, but take great care not to burn the nuts as they toast very quickly.

Nut-Flavored Pasta

It is perfectly possible to make your own pasta using nuts in the actual dough, but they must be very finely ground to produce good results. I think hazelnuts work best, and I use around one-third of nuts to two-thirds of flour. The dough may become slightly sticky as the nuts start to release their oil, so I find that it is best to rest the pasta after kneading and before it is rolled – about 30 minutes in the refrigerator with the dough in plastic wrap is sufficient. After rolling and cutting, I always leave a nut pasta to dry for an hour or so before cooking – this again makes it more manageable.

The appearance of homemade nut pasta is flecked and most attractive. While it might seem a dish suited to a whole wheat flour dough, I actually prefer the appearance of the pasta when made with white flour – the flecking from the nuts is then more apparent.

Pasta with Beans

There are several recipes in this chapter for hearty meals with both beans and pasta. These are very filling and, in my opinion, should be served with no appetizer, a side salad and just some fresh fruit to follow. That said, they make excellent dishes for informal entertaining, especially for large numbers of people. They are usually economical and not too time-consuming to prepare and most, especially the lasagnes, can be eaten with just a fork, which is ideal if guests are having to stand while they eat.

Pasta and Cheese

It is too easy to think of all Italian dishes being topped with Parmesan, and of other dishes being served in a sauce flavored with grated Cheddar. The Italians actually produce an enormous variety of cheeses, and many of them are used with pasta. Pecorino, bel paese, Gorgonzola, mozzarella and ricotta are all delicious when mixed with freshly cooked pasta, and are just a selection of the Italian cheeses that may be used. The Italians are also great ones for mixing their cheeses, and up to four are often used in one dish for a really good flavor.

The Best Parmesan

Fresh Parmesan cheese has only recently become widely available in supermarkets and delis, and it is so much fuller in flavor than the grated cheese that is available in little drums. After you have tasted the cheese "from the block," it is doubtful that you will ever be happy with anything else.

The highest grade of Parmesan is *Parmigiano Reggiano*, and it is never sold under two years old. Mature cheeses are sold between four and five years after making, and are very strong. The two-year-old Parmesan is not only for cooking – it makes the most wonderful table cheese. To keep in prime condition, wrap the cheese very tightly in plastic wrap or foil, and keep it in the refrigerator. I always think that a big block of Parmesan is one of the best souvenirs to bring home from an Italian holiday.

Pecorino – a Ewe's Milk Cheese for Pasta

The second most popular cheese for serving with pasta is pecorino. It is very similar to Parmesan, but is made from ewe's milk, and has a slightly sharp flavor. Pecorino is generally much cheaper than Parmesan as it is sold only eight months after making, so storage costs are much less. Parmesan is a cheese of northern Italy, but pecorino is made in the south and in Sardinia. I think the best pesto is made with a mixture of both.

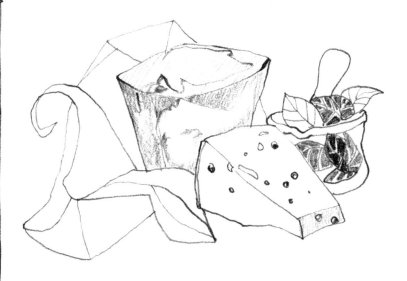

SPAGHETTI WITH SORREL AND CHEESE SAUCE

Sorrel is very similar to spinach, a vegetable that is used extensively in Italian cookery. In this recipe it produces a delicious and unusual dish.

Serves 4

INGREDIENTS
1 pound freshly cooked spaghetti
4 ounces sorrel
1¼ cups chicken or vegetable stock
1 tablespoon butter or margarine
1 tablespoon all-purpose flour
½ cup heavy cream
½ cup grated pecorino cheese
Salt and freshly ground black pepper
Pinch of cayenne pepper
2 hard-cooked eggs, roughly chopped
Grated Parmesan cheese

Cook the spaghetti to your liking. Discard any thick stems from the sorrel, then cook the leaves in the stock for 4 minutes. Melt the butter or margarine in a separate saucepan. Stir in the flour, and cook for 1 minute. Purée the sorrel in its stock in a blender or food processor, and gradually add the purée to the saucepan, stirring continuously. Bring to a boil, stirring continuously. When the sauce has thickened, stir in the cream, cheese, salt and pepper and cayenne pepper, and carefully stir in the eggs. Heat the sauce gently, and pour it over the drained pasta. Add grated Parmesan cheese before serving.

RAVIOLI WITH RICOTTA CHEESE

Ravioli are traditionally filled with meat, but cheese fillings are also popular. Ricotta is the best cheese to use, and is available in most supermarkets.

Serves 4

INGREDIENTS

Filling
2 tablespoons butter or
  margarine
1 egg yolk
1 cup ricotta cheese
½ cup grated Parmesan cheese
2 tablespoons freshly chopped
  parsley
Salt and freshly ground black
  pepper

Dough
2¼ cups white bread flour
3 eggs, lightly beaten

Tomato sauce
1 tablespoon olive oil
2 slices bacon
1 small onion, chopped
1 bay leaf
1 tablespoon freshly chopped
  basil
1 tablespoon all-purpose flour
14-ounce can chopped tomatoes
Salt and freshly ground black
  pepper
1 tablespoon heavy cream

To make the filling, beat the butter or margarine. Add the egg yolk, and beat well. Beat the ricotta cheese to a cream, and add the butter-egg mixture gradually, beating until smooth. Add the Parmesan cheese, parsley, and salt and pepper to taste. Set aside.

Prepare the dough by sifting the flour into a bowl. Make a well in the center, and add the eggs. Work the flour and eggs together with a fork, and then knead the dough by hand until smooth. Wrap in plastic wrap and let rest for 15 minutes in a cool place. Lightly flour a board, and roll the dough out thinly into a rectangle. Cut the dough in half.

Shape the filling into small balls, and set them about 1½ inches apart on one half of the dough. Put the remaining dough on top, and cut with a ravioli cutter or small cooky cutter. Seal the edges with a fork or the fingertips. Cook the ravioli in batches in a large, wide pan with plenty of boiling, salted water until tender – about 8 minutes. Remove the ravioli carefully with a draining spoon.

While the pasta is cooking, prepare the sauce. Heat the oil, and fry the bacon and onion until golden. Add the bay leaf and basil, and stir in the flour. Cook for 1 minute, then add tomatoes off the heat, stirring continuously, with salt and pepper to taste. Return the pan to the heat, and bring to a boil. Cook for 5 minutes, then press the sauce through a strainer. Stir in the cream, and adjust the seasoning to taste. Pour the tomato sauce over the ravioli, and toss gently. Serve immediately.

FARFALLE WITH CREAMY CHEESE SAUCE

Pasta in cheese sauce has long been a favorite lunch dish in our house – the farfalle give this simple dish a most attractive appearance.

Serves 4

INGREDIENTS
1 tablespoon butter or margarine
2 tablespoons all-purpose flour
1¼ cups milk
½ cup grated Gruyère or
  Cheddar cheese
½ teaspoon French mustard
10 ounces farfalle (pasta bows)
1 tablespoon grated Parmesan
  cheese

Melt the butter or margarine in a pan. Stir in the flour, and cook for 1 minute. Remove the pan from the heat, and gradually stir in the milk.

Return the pan to the heat, and stir continuously until the sauce boils. Boil for 3 minutes, then stir in the Gruyère or Cheddar cheese and mustard.

Meanwhile, cook the pasta in plenty of boiling salted water for 10 minutes, or until *al dente*. Rinse in hot water, and drain well. Pour the cheese sauce over the pasta, and toss. Top with a sprinkling of Parmesan cheese. Serve immediately.

TAGLIATELLE WITH BUTTER AND CHEESE

This recipe is simplicity itself – and wickedly delicious.

Serves 4

INGREDIENTS

10 ounces tagliatelle – preferably a mixture of yellow, green and red tagliatelle
⅓ cup butter
6 tablespoons heavy cream
½ cup grated Parmesan cheese
Salt and freshly ground black pepper

Cook the tagliatelle in a large pan of boiling salted water for 10 minutes, or until just tender, then drain. Meanwhile, put the butter and cream into a pan, and stir over a low heat until the butter has melted. Remove from the heat. Add half the grated cheese, and salt and pepper to taste. Stir into the drained tagliatelle, and serve immediately with the remaining cheese on top.

PASTA SHELLS WITH GORGONZOLA CHEESE SAUCE

Gorgonzola is one of my favorite blue cheeses for cooking – it has a sharp, tangy flavor. Only a little Parmesan is required with this dish.

Serves 4

INGREDIENTS
6 ounces Gorgonzola cheese
4 tablespoons milk
2 tablespoons butter
3 tablespoons heavy cream
Salt
10 ounces pasta shells
Grated Parmesan cheese

Heat the Gorgonzola, milk and butter gently, in a pan. Sir with a wooden spoon to make a smooth sauce, then stir in the cream, adding a little salt if necessary. Meanwhile, cook the pasta in plenty of boiling salted water for 10 minutes, or until *al dente*. Drain, shaking the colander to remove the excess water. Add the pasta to the hot sauce, and toss until well coated. Serve immediately with grated Parmesan cheese passed separately.

FONTINA CHEESE RAVIOLI

Fontina is available in most good cheese stores – the next best thing is Edam, but the flavor is not the same.

Serves 4

INGREDIENTS

2 cups all-purpose flour
3 eggs
5 ounces fontina cheese
1 tablespoon freshly chopped
  chives
1¼ cups chicken stock
1 sprig rosemary
Salt and freshly ground black
  pepper

Make the pasta by mixing together the flour and 2 of the eggs. Form into a ball, then knead until smooth and shiny. Keep in the refrigerator, wrapped, until needed. Cut the cheese into small cubes, and mix with the chives.

Roll out the dough thinly on a floured surface, and divide into two rectangles. Brush one piece with the remaining egg. Place small piles of the cheese mixture about 1½ inches apart, then cover with the remaining pasta dough. Cut into ravioli, using a small wine glass or cooky cutter, and seal the edges. Bring the stock and rosemary to a boil in a saucepan, and boil until reduced and thickened. Remove the rosemary, and season to taste.

Meanwhile, cook the ravioli in plenty of boiling, salted water for 4-5 minutes. Drain, and rinse in hot water. Serve with the reduced stock poured over.

LASAGNE WITH FOUR CHEESES

This is a well-flavored, mixed cheese lasagne, suitable for vegetarians.

Serves 4

INGREDIENTS

8 ounces green lasagne
¼ cup butter
3 tablespoons all-purpose flour
3 cups milk
⅓ cup grated Parmesan cheese
¼ cup grated Gruyère cheese
¼ cup diced mozzarella
¼ cup diced pecorino
Salt and freshly ground black pepper and nutmeg

Preheat the oven to 350°F. Cook the lasagne a few sheets at a time, in plenty of boiling, salted water. Plunge the cooked pasta into cold water, and spread out on clean dishcloths.

Melt the butter in a pan. Add the flour, and stir over a low heat for 1 minute. Remove the pan from the heat, and gradually add the milk, stirring well. Bring to a boil, stirring continuously, then add all the cheeses, except 2 tablespoons of the Parmesan, and salt, pepper and nutmeg to taste. Stir until the cheeses have melted.

Butter an ovenproof dish, and place a layer of lasagne in the bottom. Top with some of the sauce, then continue layering, finishing with a layer of sauce. Top with the reserved Parmesan, and bake for about 45 minutes, until well browned. Serve with a green salad.

TAGLIATELLE WITH BLUE CHEESE

The apricots add a touch of sweetness to this dish, and provide a dramatic contrast in flavor to the Roquefort.

Serves 4

INGREDIENTS
4 cups all-purpose flour
4-5 eggs, lightly beaten
1 tablespoon olive oil
4 ounces blue cheese (Roquefort or Stilton)
1 cup dried apricots
1¼ cups heavy cream
4 tablespoons milk
Salt and freshly ground black pepper
2 egg yolks
¼ cup pine nuts
½ bunch chives

Work together the flour and eggs to form a firm ball of dough. Knead lightly, then divide into four. Dredge each piece with flour, and flour the rollers of a pasta machine. Pass the dough through the machine. Continue rolling the pasta until thin. Thread the dough through the tagliatelle cutter, or cut into thin strips using a sharp knife. Let dry for 2 hours.

Bring a large pan of salted water to a boil with the olive oil. Cook the pasta for 2-4 minutes, stirring with a fork. Drain the tagliatelle, and rinse in plenty of cold water to prevent sticking. Set aside. Break up the cheese and force it through a strainer, using the back of a spoon. Cut the apricots into strips, then dice. Slowly heat the cream in a pan. Stir in the cheese and milk, then combine until smooth with a whisk or in a blender. Add the tagliatelle and apricots to the hot sauce, and season with salt and pepper. Heat through quickly, so as not to overcook the noodles. Mix the pasta with two forks. Remove from the heat, and mix in the egg yolks and pine nuts. Chop the chives finely, and sprinkle them over the tagliatelle. Serve immediately.

CHEESE AND TOMATO PASTA

The addition of mushrooms gives this tomato sauce just a little extra flavor. Use a mixture of Parmesan and Cheddar, if preferred.

Serves 4

·*INGREDIENTS*
8 ounces tagliatelle verdi (green)
Salt
1 tablespoon vegetable oil
1 onion, chopped
1¼ cups finely sliced mushrooms
1 tablespoon tomato paste
14-ounce can chopped tomatoes
2 tablespoons freshly chopped
   mixed herbs
1 cup grated Cheddar cheese
Freshly ground black pepper

Cook the pasta in plenty of boiling salted water for 10 minutes, or as directed on the package. Meanwhile, heat the oil, and cook the onions until they are beginning to soften. Add the mushrooms, and fry for 3 minutes. Stir in the tomato paste, tomatoes and herbs, and simmer slowly whilst the pasta cooks.

When the pasta is cooked, stir most of the cheese into the tomato sauce. Season to taste with salt and pepper. Drain the pasta, and pile it onto a serving dish. Spoon the sauce into the center, and top with the remaining cheese.

OVEN-BAKED SPAGHETTI

I make this dish by cooking too much spaghetti one day, and using the leftovers for the base of this simple oven bake.

Serves 4

INGREDIENTS
8 ounces whole wheat spaghetti, cooked
2 14-ounce cans tomatoes, roughly chopped
1 large onion, grated
1 tablespoon freshly chopped oregano
Salt and freshly ground black pepper
4 ounces Cheddar cheese
¼ cup grated Parmesan cheese

Preheat the oven to 350°F. Grease four individual ovenproof dishes, and put a quarter of the cooked spaghetti in each one. Pour the tomatoes over the top. Add the onion and oregano, and season well. Slice the Cheddar cheese finely, and arrange it over the top of the spaghetti mixture. Sprinkle with the Parmesan cheese, and bake for 30 minutes.

MACARONI AND BLUE CHEESE

Blue cheese and apples combine to make a luxurious macaroni cheese.

Serves 4

INGREDIENTS

12 ounces whole wheat macaroni
Salt
⅓ cup butter
¾ cup all-purpose flour
2½ cups milk
1 tablespoon freshly chopped tarragon
2 cups crumbled or grated blue cheese
Freshly ground black pepper
2 tablespoons vegetable oil
2 apples, cored and chopped
2 onions, chopped
1 clove garlic, crushed
Sprig of fresh tarragon, to garnish

Cook the macaroni in plenty of boiling salted water for 12 minutes, or as directed on the package, then drain well. Meanwhile, melt the butter in a saucepan. Stir in the flour, and cook for 1 minute. Remove the pan from the heat, and gradually stir in the milk. Return the pan to the heat, and cook slowly until the sauce boils and thickens, stirring continuously. Add the tarragon and blue cheese, and cook until the cheese melts. Season with salt, if needed, and freshly ground pepper.

In a smaller pan, heat the oil, and fry the apple, onion and garlic for 5 minutes, until just soft. Mix the apple and onion into the sauce, then stir in the drained pasta. Return to the heat, and warm the pasta through if necessary. Serve garnished with a sprig of fresh tarragon.

PASTA SPIRALS WITH WALNUTS AND STILTON

Walnuts and Stilton make a perfect partnership of flavors in a delicious pasta sauce.

Serves 4

INGREDIENTS
1 pound pasta spirals
Salt
1¼ cups heavy cream
1 pound Stilton cheese
1 cup walnut halves
Freshly ground black pepper
4 sprigs fresh thyme, to garnish
2 ripe figs, to garnish

Cook the pasta in plenty of boiling salted water for 10 minutes, or as directed on the package. Put the cream in a saucepan, and bring to a boil. Boil rapidly for 3 minutes; then crumble in the Stilton cheese, and stir until the cheese melts. Stir in the walnut halves, and season with pepper.

When the pasta is cooked, drain it well, then return it to the pan. Pour the sauce onto the pasta, and mix well. Serve each portion garnished with sprigs of thyme and half a ripe fig.

PENNE WITH POPPY SEEDS AND RAISINS

This is a traditional Polish dish, served on Christmas Eve.
Poppy seeds make a delicious crunchy coating on pasta.

Serves 6

INGREDIENTS
Pinch of salt
1 tablespoon oil
8 ounces penne or other pasta
 shapes
⅔ cup heavy cream
½ cup roughly ground black
 poppy seeds
2 tablespoons honey
½ cup raisins

Bring plenty of water to a boil in a large pan with a pinch of salt. Add the oil and the pasta, and return to a boil. Cook, uncovered, until tender, about 10-12 minutes. Drain and rinse the pasta under hot water. If using immediately, let drain dry. If not, put into a bowl of hot water to keep moist.

Put the cream into a deep, heavy-bottomed pan, and bring almost to a boil. When the cream is almost boiling, mix in the poppy seeds, honey and raisins. Cook slowly for about 5 minutes. The mixture should become thick, but still fall off a spoon easily. Toss the poppy seed mixture with the drained pasta, and serve hot.

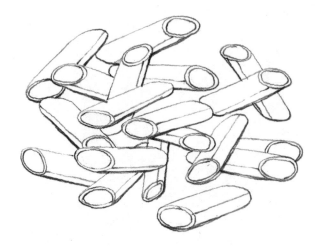

PASTA WITH BASIL AND WALNUT SAUCE

This is a classic sauce for pasta – try it once and you'll be convinced!

Serves 4

INGREDIENTS
1 cup shelled walnuts
15 basil leaves
1 small clove garlic
1 pound pasta
Olive oil
¼ cup butter
Salt and freshly ground black
    pepper

Pound together the walnuts, basil and garlic in a pestle and mortar until a smooth paste is formed. Cook the pasta in boiling salted water until tender but still firm. Rinse in hot water, and set aside to drain.

Heat a little olive oil and the butter together in a pan. Add the basil, walnut and garlic mixture, and stir well. Add the pasta to the pan. Stir well, and heat through. Check the seasoning, and add salt and pepper as necessary. Serve immediately.

PASTA SHELLS WITH AGLIATA SAUCE

The good thing about pasta shells is that they trap pools of sauce inside them, making wonderful mouthfuls of flavor.

Serves 4

INGREDIENTS
10 ounces whole wheat or plain
  pasta shells
Salt and freshly ground black
  pepper

Sauce
6 tablespoons olive oil
3 tablespoons roughly chopped
  parsley
2 cloves garlic
1 tablespoon pine kernels
1 tablespoon blanched almonds

Cook the pasta shells in a large pan of boiling salted water until just tender. Meanwhile, make the sauce. Put all the ingredients into a blender or food processor, and purée until smooth; add salt and pepper to taste. Drain the hot, cooked pasta shells, and toss together with the prepared sauce. Serve immediately.

NUTTY SPAGHETTI

A delicious, vegetarian dish which requires no extra seasoning – the peanut butter and lemon juice give plenty of flavor.

Serves 4

INGREDIENTS

8 ounces spaghetti
1 onion, finely chopped
2 tablespoons sunflower oil
2½ teaspoons curry powder
¾ cup tomato juice
3 tablespoons crunchy peanut butter
1 tablespoon lemon juice
Lemon twists and peanuts, to garnish

Cook the spaghetti in plenty of boiling, salted water until just tender, then drain well. Fry the onion in the oil until golden-brown, then stir in the curry powder, tomato juice, peanut butter and lemon juice. Simmer for 5 minutes, and then stir the sauce into the spaghetti. Garnish with lemon twists and peanuts before serving.

MACARONI WITH BASIL AND WALNUT SAUCE

Walnuts give a wonderful flavor to pasta – this dish has long been a favorite in our house, but I have to confess to adding rather more garlic than is suggested here!

Serves 4

INGREDIENTS
1 cup shelled walnuts
15 basil leaves
¼ clove garlic
1 pound macaroni
Salt and freshly ground black
　pepper
1 drop olive oil
¼ cup butter

Pound together the walnuts, basil leaves and garlic in a pestle and mortar until a smooth paste is formed.

Cook the pasta in boiling salted water for 10 minutes, or until *al dente*. Rinse in hot water, and set aside to drain.

Heat the olive oil and butter together in a saucepan. Add the basil, walnut and garlic mixture, and stir well to combine all the ingredients. Add the drained macaroni to the pan. Stir well and heat through. Check the seasoning, and add salt and pepper as necessary. Serve immediately.

SAUTÉED CHEESE KREPLACH

These cheese-stuffed kreplach are sautéed in butter until lightly browned, and then served with sour cream. They are very rich, and require only a salad to be served with them.

Serves 6-8

INGREDIENTS
1 batch Kreplach dough (see Kreplach recipe)
1 pound cottage cheese
½ cup grated Cheddar cheese
2 eggs, lightly beaten
½ teaspoon salt
½ cup melted butter
¾ cup sour cream or thick, plain yogurt
½ teaspoon paprika

Make the kreplach dough. Combine the cottage cheese, Cheddar cheese, eggs and salt in a bowl. Use the mixture to fill the kreplach, then cook the kreplach in boiling, salted water for 15 minutes.

Drain the kreplach on paper towels. Melt 2 tablespoons of the butter in a skillet, and sauté a few kreplach until lightly browned – about 3 minutes on each side. As the kreplach are cooked, pile them onto a plate, and keep warm. Use the remaining butter to sauté the rest of the kreplach in small batches. Pour some of the sour cream or yogurt over the kreplach, and serve the remainder separately. Sprinkle the kreplach with the paprika and serve.

SPAGHETTI WITH PESTO

Pesto is a very versatile sauce – it can be stirred into pasta, soups or any number of sauces and has a delicious, pungent flavor.

Serves 4

INGREDIENTS
5 tablespoons olive oil
2 cloves garlic, crushed
2 tablespoons pine nuts
2 cups fresh basil leaves
3 tablespoons grated Parmesan
  or pecorino cheese
Salt and freshly ground black
  pepper
10 ounces spaghetti
Fresh basil leaves

Heat 1 tablespoon of the oil over a low heat. Add the garlic and pine nuts, and cook until the pine nuts are a light golden-brown. Finely chop the basil leaves, pine nuts and garlic in a food processor with a metal blade, or in a blender. When smooth, add the remaining oil in a thin stream, blending continuously. Transfer the mixture to a bowl, and stir in the cheese, adding salt and pepper to taste.

Meanwhile, cook the spaghetti in a large pan of boiling salted water for 10 minutes, or until just tender. Drain, and serve with the pesto tossed through the pasta. Serve with a side dish of grated cheese, and garnish with fresh basil.

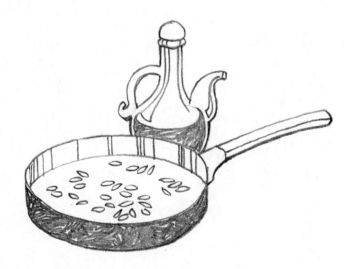

TAGLIATELLE WITH FRESH BASIL SAUCE

This basil sauce is less rich than a traditional pesto, as it does not include any pine nuts. It is very rich, a meal in itself, but may also be served with cold roast meat.

Serves 4

INGREDIENTS
1 pound tagliatelle
20 fresh basil leaves
1 clove garlic
¼ cup grated Parmesan cheese
4 tablespoons olive oil
2 tablespoons butter
Salt and freshly ground black pepper

Cook the pasta in boiling salted water until tender but still firm. Drain, and rinse; then set aside to drain. Pound the basil leaves in a pestle and mortar. Add the garlic, and pound until well mixed. Add the Parmesan cheese to a large bowl, and whisk in the olive oil. Add the butter to the pasta. Put over a low heat, and add the basil sauce. Stir well with a wooden spoon, and season with salt and pepper. Serve as soon as the pasta is completely heated through.

SPAGHETTI ALLA GENOVESE

*The use of less basil and addition of parsley makes this sauce
slightly less expensive than the very similar pesto sauce.*

Serves 4

INGREDIENTS

½ cup fresh basil leaves
½ cup fresh parsley
1 clove garlic, crushed
4 tablespoons pine nuts or
  chopped walnuts
½ cup grated Parmesan cheese
Salt and freshly ground black
  pepper
⅔ cup olive oil
1 pound spaghetti, freshly
  cooked

Combine the basil, parsley, garlic, nuts, cheese, and salt and pepper in a food processor or blender, and work until finely chopped. With the machine running, pour the oil through the funnel in a thin, steady stream. Process until smooth, with the consistency of mayonnaise. Pour the sauce over the freshly cooked pasta, and toss to serve. Serve with additional grated cheese if wished.

TAGLIATELLE WITH PINE NUTS

This is a piquant recipe, suitable for vegetarians, but popular with meat eaters too! The pine nuts give a slightly crunchy texture to the dish.

Serves 4

INGREDIENTS
12 ounces tagliatelle
Salt
6 tablespoons olive oil
1 large onion, sliced
1 clove garlic, crushed
1 cup pine nuts
14-ounce can artichoke hearts, drained
2 tablespoons freshly chopped parsley
Grated Parmesan cheese

Cook the tagliatelle in plenty of lightly salted boiling water for 10 minutes, or until *al dente*. Just before the tagliatelle is cooked, heat the oil in a skillet, and fry the onion and garlic until starting to brown. Add the pine nuts, and cook for 1 minute; then add the artichoke hearts and parsley. Heat slowly for a few minutes. Drain the tagliatelle well, and add it to the pan; toss until the tagliatelle is well coated in the oil. Stir in a generous handful of grated Parmesan cheese. Transfer to a warmed serving dish, and scatter with a little more grated Parmesan cheese. Serve immediately.

SPAGHETTI RICE

*This is a filling and unusual dish – I would serve it with a
tossed green salad.*

Serves 4

INGREDIENTS

4 ounces long-grain rice
4 ounces spaghetti, broken into
  2-inch pieces
3 tablespoons oil
4 tablespoons sesame seeds
2 tablespoons freshly chopped
  chives
Salt and freshly ground black
  pepper
2 cups chicken, beef or vegetable
  stock
1 tablespoon soy sauce
2 tablespoons freshly chopped
  parsley

Rinse the rice and pasta to
remove any starch, and let drain.
Heat the oil in a large skillet or
wok, and add the rice and pasta.
Cook over a medium heat to
brown slightly, stirring
continuously. Add the sesame
seeds, and cook until the rice,
pasta and seeds are golden-
brown. Add the chives, salt and
pepper, and 1¼ cups of the
stock. Stir in the soy sauce, and
bring to a boil. Cover the pan,
and cook for about 20 minutes,
or until the rice and pasta are
tender and the stock is absorbed.
Add more of the reserved stock
as necessary. Do not let the rice
and pasta dry out during
cooking. Fluff up the grains of
rice with a fork, and sprinkle
with the parsley before serving.

BEAN SALAD

Crispy bacon adds flavor and texture to this bean and pasta salad. It is an excellent dish to serve as part of a buffet.

Serves 4

INGREDIENTS
8 ounces macaroni
2 rindless bacon slices, chopped
1 onion, chopped
1-2 tablespoons wine vinegar
3-4 tablespoons olive oil
1 teaspoon freshly chopped parsley
Salt and freshly ground black pepper
15-ounce can red kidney beans, drained
2 celery stalks, sliced diagonally

Cook the macaroni in plenty of salted, boiling water for 10 minutes, or until tender but still firm. Rinse in cold water, and drain well. Heat a skillet, and sauté the bacon in its own fat until crisp. Add the onion, and cook until soft.

Mix together the vinegar, oil and parsley, and season well. Add the bacon, onion, kidney beans and celery to the macaroni. Pour the dressing over the salad, and toss together. Chill briefly before serving.

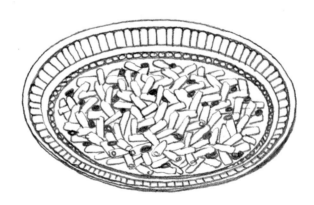

SPAGHETTI WITH KIDNEY BEANS AND PESTO

Pesto is a glorious Italian sauce of basil, garlic and pine nuts blended with olive oil – it often has Parmesan and pecorino cheeses added to it as well. Store the sauce in a screw-top jar in the refrigerator for up to a week, and add the sauce to pasta, rice and meat dishes.

Serves 4

INGREDIENTS
Pesto Sauce
1 large bunch fresh basil
4 cloves garlic, crushed
3 tablespoons pine nuts
⅔ cup extra virgin olive oil
1 tablespoon lemon juice
Salt and freshly ground black
   pepper

8 ounces spaghetti
Salt and freshly ground black
   pepper
1 small onion, finely chopped
2 tablespoons olive oil
1 clove garlic, crushed
2 teaspoons pesto sauce
1½ cups cooked red kidney
   beans, or 15-ounce can,
   drained

Garnish
Sprigs of fresh basil

Prepare the sauce. Put all the ingredients into a blender or food processor, and work until fairly smooth; the sauce should still retain a little texture.

Bring a large pan of salted water to a boil. Add the spaghetti, and cook for 10 minutes, or until *al dente*. Meanwhile, fry the onion slowly in the olive oil for 3 minutes; mix in the garlic and the pesto sauce. Drain the spaghetti thoroughly, and add it to the onion and pesto mixture, together with the red kidney beans. Stir over a low heat for 1-2 minutes, then serve piping hot, garnished with basil.

BEANY LASAGNE

Lasagne makes an ideal dish for vegetarians. It usually contains lentils, but this recipe is made with aduki beans, giving a nutty flavor and texture.

Serves 4-6

INGREDIENTS
8 sheets whole wheat lasagne
1 large onion, finely chopped
1 tablespoon olive oil
1-2 cloves garlic, crushed
cooked aduki beans
1 green bell pepper, chopped
14-ounce can chopped tomatoes
1 tablespoon tomato paste
1 teaspoon dried basil
1 teaspoon dried oregano
Salt and freshly ground black
pepper

Sauce
2 tablespoons margarine or
butter
¼ cup whole wheat flour
2 cups milk
½ cup grated Cheddar cheese
(optional)
Salt and freshly ground black
pepper

Cook the lasagne in a large pan of boiling, salted water for 8-10 minutes. Drain well, and spread out on clean dishcloths until required. Cook the onion in the oil until soft but not browned. Add the crushed garlic, then the beans, green bell pepper, chopped tomatoes, tomato paste and herbs. Season and simmer for about 10 minutes, or until the vegetables are tender.

Preheat the oven to 350°F. To make the sauce, combine the margarine or butter, flour and cold milk. Gradually bring to a boil, stirring continuously. When thickened, let simmer slowly for about 6 minutes; then stir in the cheese, and season to taste. Spoon half the bean and vegetable mixture into a greased ovenproof dish, and top with half the lasagne. Repeat the layers, and top with the cheese sauce. Bake for 35 minutes, or until golden-brown and bubbling. Serve immediately.

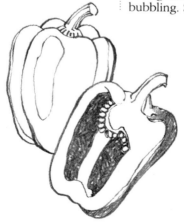

PASTA WITH FISH

Perhaps pasta shells are amongst the most popular of dried pasta shapes because of the Italian passion for pasta with seafood sauces! I have absolutely no proof to support my theory, but there are an amazing number of pasta recipes which include fish.

Quick-Cook Partners

One of the great advantages of meals based on pasta is that they are very quick to prepare, and require a relatively short cooking time. Of course there are complicated dishes with intricate garnishes or presentation, and these will take longer than most pasta dishes to prepare, but the vast majority are quick. Fish and seafood are therefore ideal ingredients for pasta sauces as they are so much quicker to cook than the majority of meats, and yet yield the same high protein value in the finished dish.

Clams – A Favorite with Pasta

The first clams that I ever tasted were in a dish of pasta with a seafood sauce. They are molluscs, like oysters and mussels, and have a hinged shell which opens during cooking to reveal the clam inside. Any shells that do not open should, like mussels, be discarded, as the clam inside is dead and not to be eaten. Clams are popular throughout the world, but especially in the Mediterranean region. They are often cultivated in the same pools as oysters, and some of the largest clam beds are in France and Portugal. They are ideal molluscs to use in pasta dishes, especially with the thinner shapes such as spaghetti and tagliatelle, as they are relatively small and therefore mix in well. They are also most attractive, having small round shells of a light sandy brown color.

I always think that mussels look stunning in risottos and paellas, but clams are better in pasta dishes. They are found, or cultivated, in the wet sand of freshwater streams and coasts, and therefore require careful washing to remove the sand. When buying live clams they are best treated as for mussels. Put them into a large bowl of lightly salted water, and sprinkle a little flour or oatmeal on the surface – this encourages the molluscs to clean themselves, flushing the sand out of their shells.

A Garnish Comes into its Own

Anchovies have long been popular the world over as a salty seasoning and garnish for robust dishes that are absolutely loaded with flavor. Many Italian and Mediterranean French recipes are good examples of these strong partnerships of flavors, mixing anchovies with olives, tomatoes, herbs and capers to give pungent and tongue-tingling sauces. Some people do, however, find the anchovies just a little too salty, but soaking the fillets in a little milk before use will tone down the saltiness.

The recipe for Macaroni Cheese with Anchovies is a classic example of these small fish being used as both a seasoning and a garnish. A word of advice, however, on garnishes. Use a very sharp, smooth-bladed knife to cut the anchovy fillets lengthwise, making elegant thin strips which look much neater than using the whole fillets for garnish. However, as I am a fan of the strong, salty taste of the anchovy, I love recipes such as the Penne with Anchovy Sauce, where a paste of the fish is mixed with tomatoes to give a strong, pungent sauce. The anchovies must be mixed with another ingredient, as they would be far too strong a flavor by themselves.

Seafood Lasagne – Light but Filling

I often make a seafood lasagne for friends who do not eat meat. I find it an almost perfect dish for entertaining as it is colorful and full of flavor, and just a little unusual. There are two dramatically different lasagne recipes in this chapter, one with a mixture of shellfish and the other, an elegant dish with salmon and fennel. I also often use smoked haddock and chopped hard-cooked eggs. However, a word of advice when preparing seafood lasagne, especially when made with fillets of fish. Do try to remove as many bones as possible because, in my experience, people just plough through lasagne expecting all the work to have been done for them. A friend of mine recently had a bone in her throat from my smoked haddock lasagne, which was most embarrassing because she had to spend the next morning at the local hospital. It isn't always possible to remove all the bones during the preparation, so do warn your friends if you think there might be some in the dish.

TAGLIATELLE WITH EGGS AND LUMPFISH

This is light and sophisticated – add a splash of vodka just before serving for special occasions.

Serves 2, or 4 as an appetizer

INGREDIENTS
4 small eggs, hard-cooked
8 ounces red tagliatelle
¼ cup butter or margarine
Freshly ground black pepper
¼ cup salmon (keta) or red
  lumpfish roe

Remove the shells from the hard-cooked eggs. Cut in half, and scoop out the yolks with a teaspoon. Press the yolks through a strainer. Rinse the egg whites, and cut them into strips.

Cook the tagliatelle in plenty of boiling salted water until *al dente*. Rinse in hot water, and drain well. Melt the butter or margarine in a pan, and add freshly ground black pepper and the tagliatelle. Add the egg white strips, and toss well. Sprinkle the salmon or lumpfish roe over, and top with the strained egg yolks. Serve immediately.

TUNA CANNELLONI

Cannelloni are easy to prepare, but rinse the tubes well after boiling, to prevent them from sticking together.

Serves 4

INGREDIENTS
12 cannelloni shells

Filling
2 tablespoons butter or
    margarine
1 onion, chopped
1 cup chopped mushrooms
1 stalk celery, chopped
1 tablespoon all-purpose flour
⅔ cup milk
4 tablespoons heavy cream
4 tablespoons mayonnaise
1 tablespoon freshly chopped
    oregano
7-ounce can tuna
Salt and freshly ground black
    pepper
3 shallots, chopped
1 egg, lightly beaten

Topping
4 tablespoons fresh bread
    crumbs
½ cup grated cheese
1 tablespoon butter or margarine

Preheat the oven to 375°F. Cook the cannelloni shells in a large pan of boiling salted water for 15-20 minutes, until tender. Rinse in hot water, and drain well.

Meanwhile, melt the butter or margarine for the filling in a saucepan. Add the onion, and cook until transparent; then add the mushrooms and celery, and cook for 5 minutes Stir in the flour, and cook until light golden-brown. Gradually add the milk, stirring continuously. Bring to a boil, and cook for 3 minutes, stirring all the time. Add the cream, mayonnaise, oregano and the undrained flaked tuna. Season with salt and pepper, and stir until boiling; then simmer for 3 minutes. Add the shallots and egg, and mix well.

Spoon the mixture into the cannelloni shells, and put them into an ovenproof dish. Mix the bread crumbs and cheese together, and scatter over the cannelloni; then dot with the butter or margarine. Bake for 20 minutes. Serve immediately.

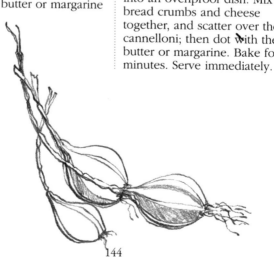

PASTA WITH LEEKS AND MUSSELS

Mussels and leeks combine well in this tasty lunch dish.

Serves 6

INGREDIENTS
1 pound fresh mussels
½ cup white wine
1 shallot, chopped
2 leeks
¾ cup heavy cream
Salt and freshly ground black
  pepper
1 pound pasta spirals
1 tablespoon oil
2 slices cooked ham
¼ cup butter
Freshly chopped chives to
  garnish

Scrub the mussels; remove the beards, and wash in several changes of water to remove any sand. In a large, covered saucepan, cook the mussels in the white wine with the chopped shallot for about 5 minutes, over a high heat. Cook, and remove the opened mussels from their shells. Discard any that have not opened. Reserve the cooking liquid.

Quarter each leek lengthwise. Wash thoroughly, and slice finely. In a covered saucepan, cook the leeks in the cream, with salt and pepper to taste, for 10 minutes over a low heat. Cook the pasta in a large pan of boiling, salted water with the oil. Stir the pasta occasionally as it cooks, to prevent it from sticking. Drain after 5-6 minutes, and rinse in cold water. Remove any fat or rind from the ham, and cut it into small pieces.

Drain the mussel liquor through a strainer lined with cheesecloth. Measure out about ⅔ cup. Add the shelled mussels and the measured mussel liquor to the cream mixture, and cook for 4 minutes, stirring continuously. Melt the butter in a deep skillet, and reheat the pasta over a low heat with the ham. Season to taste. When the pasta is heated through, add the cream and leek sauce, and serve garnished with the chopped chives.

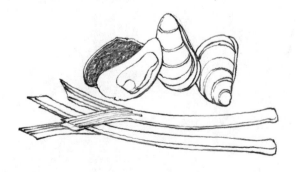

SMOKED HADDOCK WITH PEAS AND PASTA

Smoked haddock is my favorite fish to serve with pasta.

Serves 4

INGREDIENTS

1¼ cups milk
8 ounces smoked haddock fillets, skinned
2 tablespoons butter or margarine
¼ cup all-purpose flour
1 tablespoon freshly chopped chives
1 tablespoon freshly chopped parsley
⅓ cup peas, cooked
1 hard-cooked egg, chopped
Salt and freshly ground black pepper
8 ounces pasta shells, cooked

Heat the milk slowly in a large skillet, which has a tight-fitting lid. Add the fish when the milk is warm. Cover the pan, and poach the fish slowly for about 8 minutes. Check the pan occasionally, adding a little more milk if necessary. When cooked, drain the fish, reserving the milk.

Melt the butter or margarine and stir in the flour. Heat slowly for a few minutes. Add the reserved milk, stirring continuously. Heat until the sauce boils and thickens; if it is too thick, add a little more milk. Add the chives and parsley to the sauce, and pour it into a large bowl. Flake the fish, removing any bones. Add the fish to the sauce, along with the peas, hard-cooked egg, and salt and pepper. Stir well; then add the drained pasta to the sauce mixture, and again mix gently to distribute the fish through the pasta and sauce. Return the mixture to a large saucepan, and heat slowly for 3-4 minutes. Serve immediately.

SHELL PASTA WITH TARAMASALATA

Homemade taramasalata is delicious – used as a sauce for freshly cooked pasta, it is rich and most unusual.

Serves 4

INGREDIENTS
Taramasalata
8 slices white bread, crusts removed
4 tablespoons milk
8 ounces smoked cod's roe
½ onion, grated
6 tablespoons olive oil
2 teaspoons lemon juice
Freshly ground black pepper

8 ounces shell pasta
2 tablespoons lemon juice
1 tablespoon caviar or black lumpfish roe
10 black olives, pitted and chopped

To make the taramasalata, crumble the bread into a bowl, and add the milk. Set aside to soak. Scoop the cod's roe out of its skin, and break it down with a wooden spoon. Squeeze the bread dry in a strainer. Add the onion and bread to the roe, and mix well. Add the oil and lemon juice very gradually, alternating between the two. Beat until smooth and creamy. Add pepper to taste, and salt if necessary.

Cook the pasta shells in lots of boiling, salted water for 10 minutes, or until *al dente*. Rinse in hot water, and drain well. Sprinkle the lemon juice over the pasta, and toss with the taramasalata. Garnish with caviar or lumpfish roe and black olives. Serve immediately.

CURRIED SHRIMP SALAD

I particularly like this shrimp pasta salad – the small soup pasta blends well with the shrimp to make an evenly textured dish.

Serves 4

INGREDIENTS
2 tablespoons olive oil
1 clove garlic, crushed
1 small onion, chopped
1 tablespoon curry powder
1 teaspoon paprika
1 teaspoon tomato paste
⅔ cup water
2 slices lemon
Salt and freshly ground black pepper
1 teaspoon apricot jam
1¼ cups mayonnaise
8 ounces small pasta shapes for soup
Juice of ½ lemon
8 ounces cooked shrimp, shelled and deveined

Heat the oil, and fry the garlic and onion slowly until soft but not browned. Add the curry powder and paprika, and cook over a low heat for 2 minutes. Stir in the tomato paste and water, then add the lemon slices, and salt and pepper to taste. Cook slowly for 10 minutes, then stir in the jam. Bring to a boil, and simmer for 2 minutes. Strain the mixture, and let cool. Add the mayonnaise.

Meanwhile, cook the pasta in plenty of boiling, salted water for 10 minutes, or until tender but still firm. Rinse under cold water, and drain well. Toss the pasta in the lemon juice, and put into a serving dish. Arrange the shrimp on top, and pour the curry sauce over. Toss well. Sprinkle with paprika before serving. Chill briefly if necessary.

NIÇOIS SALAD

A variation on the classic Salade Niçoise. I usually serve this on a bed of crisp lettuce.

Serves 4

INGREDIENTS

8 ounces penne
7-ounce can tuna fish, drained and flaked
3 tomatoes, quartered
½ cucumber, cut into batons
4 ounces green beans, cooked
12 black olives, halved and pitted
2-ounce can anchovy fillets, drained, and soaked in milk if wished to remove saltiness
Salt and freshly ground black pepper
½ cup French dressing

Cook the penne in plenty of boiling, salted water until tender, but still firm, about 10 minutes. Rinse in cold water, drain and let dry.

Put the flaked tuna in the bottom of a salad dish. Toss the pasta with the tomatoes, cucumber, green beans, olives and anchovies. Add a little salt and pepper to taste. Pour the French dressing over the salad, and mix together with the tuna.

SHRIMP SALAD

This recipe makes a very quick lunch dish for two or an appetizer for four.

Serves 2-4

INGREDIENTS
8 ounces pasta shells
Juice of 1 lemon
1 teaspoon paprika
⅔ cup mayonnaise
8 ounces cooked shrimp, shelled and deveined
Salt and freshly ground black pepper
1 lettuce
1 English cucumber, sliced

Cook the pasta in plenty of boiling, salted water for 10 minutes, or until tender. Drain and rinse under cold water. Shake off any excess water. Put the pasta into a bowl, and add the lemon juice. Let cool.

Mix the paprika into the mayonnaise, and add the shrimp and seasoning, then mix gently. Arrange a bed of lettuce leaves and sliced cucumber in a dish, and pile the pasta into the center with the shrimp on top.

TUNA AND TOMATO SALAD

This makes a substantial salad to serve with a lettuce garnish or as part of a cold buffet.

Serves 4

INGREDIENTS
1 tablespoon freshly chopped basil
6 tablespoons French dressing
12 ounces pasta shapes of your choice
6 tomatoes
1½ cups drained and flaked, canned (preferably in brine) tuna fish

Mix the fresh basil with the French dressing in a small jug or bowl. Cook the pasta shapes in a large saucepan of boiling, lightly salted water, until they are tender. This takes about 10 minutes. Rinse the pasta in cold water, and drain well, shaking to remove any excess water.

Put the pasta shapes into a large bowl, and toss with 3 tablespoons of the French dressing, mixing well to insure that they are evenly coated. Let cool. Slice enough tomatoes to arrange around the outside of the serving dish, and then chop the rest. Put the chopped tomatoes into another bowl, and add the remaining French dressing. Pile into the center of the serving dish.

Add the flaked tuna to the pasta shapes, and toss together gently. Pile the pasta and tuna over the chopped tomatoes in the center of the dish, and arrange the tomato slices around the edge. Chill well until required.

PASTA SHELLS WITH SEAFOOD

I love any dish combining pasta and seafood. The shrimp in this become trapped in the pasta shells, producing lovely mouthfuls of flavor!

Serves 4

INGREDIENTS

¼ cup butter or margarine
2 cloves garlic, crushed
5 tablespoons dry white wine
1¼ cups light cream
1 tablespoon cornstarch
2 tablespoons water
1 tablespoon lemon juice
Salt and freshly ground black
    pepper
10 ounces pasta shells
1 pound raw shrimp, shelled and
    deveined
4 ounces scallops, cleaned and
    sliced
1 tablespoon freshly chopped
    parsley

Melt the butter or margarine in a pan. Add the garlic, and cook for 1 minute; then add the wine and cream. Bring to a boil, and cook for 2 minutes. Mix the cornstarch with the water, and pour it into the sauce. Stir until boiling, then add the lemon juice, and salt and pepper to taste.

Meanwhile, cook the pasta in plenty of boiling, salted water, until tender – about 10 minutes. Drain, shaking to remove excess water. Add the shrimp and scallops to the sauce, and cook for 3-4 minutes, or until just cooked through. Pour the sauce over the pasta shells, and toss. Garnish with parsley before serving.

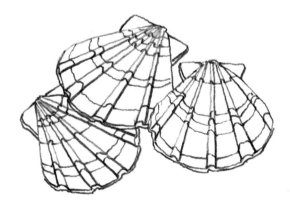

FISH RAVIOLI

Ravioli stuffed with fish is quite unusual. The lemon sauce really makes this dish.

Serves 4

INGREDIENTS

Filling
8 ounces white fish fillets, skinned and boned
1 slice of onion
1 slice of lemon
6 peppercorns
1 bay leaf
1 tablespoon lemon juice
1¼ cups water
2 eggs, beaten
2 tablespoons fresh bread crumbs
1 scallion, finely chopped
Salt and freshly ground black pepper

Dough
2¼ cups white bread flour
Pinch of salt
3 eggs, lightly beaten

Lemon sauce
2 tablespoons butter or margarine
¼ cup all-purpose flour
1¼ cups strained cooking liquor from the fish
2 tablespoons heavy cream
Salt and freshly ground black pepper
2 tablespoons lemon juice

Preheat the oven to 350°F. Wash and dry the fish. Place in an ovenproof dish with the slices of onion and lemon, the peppercorns, bay leaf, lemon juice and water. Cover the dish, and cook in the oven for 20 minutes. Remove the fish with a draining spoon. Strain the liquor,

and set aside. When the fish is cool, beat it with the back of a spoon to a pulp. Add the eggs, bread crumbs, scallion and salt and pepper to taste, then mix well.

Sift the flour into a bowl, and add the salt. Make a well in the center, and add the eggs. Work the flour and eggs together with a spoon, and then knead by hand, until a smooth dough is formed. Let rest for 15 minutes. Lightly flour a board, and roll out the dough thinly into a rectangle. Cut the dough in half. Shape the filling into small balls, and set them about 1½ inches apart on one half of the dough. Lay the other half on top, and cut with a ravioli cutter or small cooky cutter. Seal the edges with a fork. Cook the ravioli in batches in a large pan of boiling, salted water until tender – about 8 minutes. Remove carefully with a draining spoon.

Meanwhile, make the sauce. Melt the butter or margarine in a pan. Stir in the flour, and cook for 30 seconds. Take the pan off the heat, and gradually stir in the liquor from the cooked fish. Return to the heat, and bring to a boil. Simmer for 4 minutes, stirring continuously; add the cream, and mix well. Season to taste. Remove from the heat, and gradually stir in the lemon juice. Do not reboil. Pour the sauce over the hot ravioli, and serve.

TAGLIATELLE WITH SMOKED SALMON AND CAVIAR

This is affordable luxury! I can never decide which color tagliatelle I like best in this dish.

Serves 4

INGREDIENTS

8 ounces green tagliatelle
2 tablespoons butter or margarine
Juice of ½ lemon
Freshly ground black pepper
3 ounces smoked salmon, cut into strips
2 tablespoons heavy cream
¼ cup caviar, salmon or red lumpfish roe

Garnish
Lemon slices

Cook the tagliatelle in plenty of boiling, salted water for 10 minutes, or until tender but still firm. Rinse under hot water, and drain well.

Melt the butter or margarine in a pan, and add the lemon juice and freshly ground black pepper; then add the tagliatelle and smoked salmon and toss together. Serve, topped with the cream and a sprinkling of red caviar. Garnish with lemon slices.

SPAGHETTI PESCATORE

This recipe uses a wide selection of shellfish, but you can use whatever is available. The oysters add a touch of luxury, but are not essential.

Serves 4

INGREDIENTS
8 mussels
12 small clams
8 ounces cod fillets
4 ounces squid, cleaned
2 tablespoons olive oil
4 jumbo shrimps, cooked
4 fresh oysters
1 cup dry white wine
3 cups tomato sauce
2 tablespoons tomato paste
½ green bell pepper, diced
Salt and freshly ground black
    pepper
8 ounces spaghetti
Freshly chopped parsley
    (optional)

Prepare the seafood. If using fresh mussels, clean the closed shellfish, removing any beards, and cook in boiling water for 5 minutes until opened. (Discard any that remain closed.) Let cool, then remove the mussels and clams from their shells, keeping a few in shells for garnish if wished. Skin and bone the cod, and cut the fish into ½-inch pieces. Cut the squid into rings.

Heat the olive oil in a pan, and add the squid. Fry gently until white, then add the wine, tomato sauce and paste, green bell pepper, and salt and pepper to taste. Simmer for 20 minutes, then add the cod. Simmer for an additional 10 minutes, stirring occasionally. Add the clams and mussels. When the mixture reboils, adjust the seasoning to taste. Add the jumbo shrimps and oysters slowly and heat.

Meanwhile, cook the spaghetti in plenty of boiling salted water for 10 minutes, or until tender but still firm. Drain well. Add the seafood sauce, and toss together. Garnish with freshly chopped parsley if wished.

CARRETTIERA WITH PASTA RINGS

I sometimes add a few cooked peas to this for extra color, and a little garlic for extra flavor.

Serves 4

INGREDIENTS
2 tablespoons butter or margarine
1½ cups sliced mushrooms
7-ounce can tuna, flaked
Salt and freshly ground black pepper
9 ounces pasta rings

Melt the butter or margarine in a pan. Add the mushrooms, and cook for 2-3 minutes. Add the flaked tuna and seasoning to taste, then heat slowly.

Meanwhile, cook the pasta in plenty of boiling, salted water for 10 minutes, or until tender but still firm. Rinse in hot water, and drain well. Add the sauce to the cooked pasta, and toss together. Serve immediately.

SPAGHETTI MARINARA

I always enjoy a fish sauce with pasta – it makes a change from the more traditional meat sauces, and is slightly lighter. This is one of my favorite summer recipes.

Serves 4

Ingredients

2-ounce can anchovy fillets
5 tablespoons water
5 tablespoons dry white wine
1 bay leaf
4 peppercorns
8 ounces scallops, cleaned and sliced
2 tablespoons olive oil
2 cloves garlic, crushed
1 tablespoon freshly chopped basil
14-ounce can chopped tomatoes
1 tablespoon tomato paste
10 ounces spaghetti
1 pound cooked shrimp, shelled and deveined
2 tablespoons freshly chopped parsley
Salt and freshly ground black pepper

Drain the anchovies, and cut them into small pieces. Put the water, wine, bay leaf and peppercorns into a pan, and bring to a slow boil. Add the scallops, and poach for 2 minutes. Remove the scallops with a draining spoon and, let drain.

Heat the oil in a separate pan. Add the garlic and basil, and cook for 30 seconds. Add the tomatoes, chopped anchovies and tomato paste. Stir until combined, then cook for 10 minutes.

Meanwhile, bring a large pan of salted water to a boil. Add the spaghetti, and cook for 10 minutes, or until *al dente*; then drain. Add the shrimp and scallops to the sauce, and cook for 1 minute longer. Add 1 tablespoon of the parsley, and stir. Season with salt and pepper to taste. Pour the sauce over the spaghetti, and serve immediately, sprinkled with the remaining parsley.

CRAB CANNELLONI

*An easy way to fill the cannelloni tubes is to place the filling
in a piping bag fitted with a large, plain tip, then pipe the
mixture into the pasta.*

Serves 4

INGREDIENTS
12 cannelloni shells

Filling
2 tablespoons butter or
  margarine
3 shallots, chopped
225g/8oz crab meat
½ teaspoon Worcestershire sauce
1 teaspoon Dijon mustard
Salt and freshly ground black
  pepper

Mornay Sauce
2 tablespoons butter or
  margarine
¼ cup all-purpose flour
1¼ cups milk
¼ cup grated Parmesan cheese
Salt and freshly ground black
  pepper

Preheat the oven to 400°F. Cook
the cannelloni shells in a large
pan of boiling salted water for
15-20 minutes, or until *al dente*.
Rinse in hot water, and drain
well.

Meanwhile, melt the butter or
margarine for the filling in a pan.
Add the shallots, crab meat,
Worcestershire sauce, mustard,
and salt and pepper, then stir
until heated through. Fill the
cannelloni shells with the crab
mixture, and put them into a
greased ovenproof dish.

Melt the butter for the sauce in a
pan, and stir in the flour. Remove
from the heat, and gradually add
the milk. Return the pan to the
heat, and bring the sauce to a
boil; cook for 3 minutes, stirring
continuously. Stir in half the
cheese until it melts, then season
with salt and pepper. Pour the
sauce over the cannelloni, and
sprinkle with the remaining
cheese. Bake for 10-15 minutes,
or put under a hot broiler until
brown. Serve immediately.

SEAFOOD WITH EGG NOODLES

This recipe may be made with thread egg noodles or with tagliatelle – I like to use the finer noodles as the dish has a taste of the Orient.

Serves 4

INGREDIENTS

1 pound mixed seafood, such as shrimp, white fish fillets, squid, clams and mussels
3 large green chilis, seeded and chopped
1 tablespoon freshly chopped cilantro leaves
2 cloves garlic, crushed
6 ounces egg noodles
2 tablespoons oil
4 ounces snow peas
8 baby corn cobs
½ red bell pepper, sliced
1 tablespoon fish sauce
⅔ cup fish stock
1 tablespoon lime juice
2 teaspoons cornstarch

Cook the seafood separately in boiling water until cooked through, then drain and set aside. If using squid, score the hoods in a diamond pattern before cutting into pieces. Pound the chilis, cilantro and garlic together in a pestle and mortar. Cook the noodles as directed on the package. Heat the oil in a wok or heavy-bottomed skillet. Add the snow peas, baby corn and bell pepper, and stir-fry for 4 minutes. Add the chili mixture and fish sauce, and cook for 2 minutes. Stir in the fish stock, and add the cooked seafood and noodles to the pan. Mix the lime juice and cornstarch together; stir into the wok, and cook until boiling and thickened.

PASTA WITH CLAMS

*Unless you live on the coast, you will probably have difficulty
in finding clams in their shells. Use 1-1½ cups shelled clams,
but make certain that they have not been pickled in brine.*

Serves 4

INGREDIENTS
1 pound clams
½ cup white wine
1 shallot, chopped
11 ounces spaghetti
¼ cup butter
1 clove garlic, chopped
1 tablespoon freshly chopped
  parsley
Salt and freshly ground black
  pepper

Put the clams into a large pan.
Add the white wine and shallot,
and set over a high heat. Shake
the pan frequently until the
clams are open. Remove from
the heat, and set the pan aside
until the clams are cool enough
to handle, then remove them
from their shells.

Cook the pasta in boiling salted
water until tender but still firm.
Rinse in hot water, and set aside
to drain. Melt the butter in a
saucepan, and add the garlic,
chopped parsley, pasta and
clams. Season with salt and
pepper. Cook until the pasta is
heated through. Serve
immediately.

SALMON AND FENNEL LASAGNE

Salmon and fennel make a luxurious lasagne for a special occasion.

Serves 4

INGREDIENTS
2½ cups all-purpose flour
3 eggs, beaten
2 tablespoons butter
2 tablespoons all-purpose flour
1¼ cups milk
1¼ pounds salmon (in one long piece if possible)
1 teaspoon fennel seeds
Salt and freshly ground black pepper
1 cup fish stock
⅓ cup grated Gruyère cheese

Make the dough by mixing together the 2½ cups flour and the eggs. Knead well, and set the dough aside to rest for 30 minutes. Roll out very thinly into long strips. Part-cook the pasta in boiling salted water for 1 minute. Drain and then lay out on damp dishcloths, without overlapping the strips.

Preheat the oven to 375°F. Melt the butter in a saucepan, and stir in the 2 tablespoons flour. Cook slowly for 1 minute. Remove from the heat, and gradually add the milk. Return the pan to the heat, and bring the sauce to a boil. Cook for 3 minutes, stirring continuously.

Cut the salmon into long thin slices similar to smoked salmon slices – a very sharp knife with a finely serrated blade is best for this delicate job. Remove all the bones. Butter an ovenproof dish, and lay some strips of pasta into the bottom. Build up layers of the white sauce, a few fennel seeds, the salmon, salt and pepper, and then another layer of pasta. Continue layering, finishing with a layer of pasta. Add the fish stock, and top with the cheese. Cook in the oven until the fish stock has been almost completely absorbed, about 20-25 minutes. Serve hot.

SPAGHETTI WITH CRAB AND BACON

Bacon and crab combine well to make a really flavorsome and luxurious dish.

Serves 4

INGREDIENTS
1 bunch parsley
4 cups all-purpose flour
4 eggs, lightly beaten
8 ounces bacon, in one piece
1 tablespoon olive oil
1½ cups crab meat
1¼ cups heavy cream
3 tablespooons butter
Salt and freshly ground black pepper
Freshly chopped chervil

Trim the leaves off the parsley. Cook for 10 minutes in boiling water, then press the parsley through a fine strainer. Reserve the cooking liquid. Purée the parsley with 3 tablespoons of the cooking liquid in a blender or food processor. Mix together the flour, eggs and 1½ tablespoons of the parsley purée. Knead lightly, then form into a ball. Divide the dough into four, and form these pieces into balls. Press each ball flat, and run it through a pasta machine, until thinly rolled. Pass through the spaghetti cutter, or cut finely with a sharp knife.

Cut the rind off the bacon, and cut the meat into strips, then into small dice. Add the olive oil to a large pan of boiling salted water, and cook the spaghetti for 5 minutes. Strain and rinse in hot water. Shred the crab; then add it to the cream and heat slowly. Meanwhile, melt the butter in a pan; when it bubbles, add the bacon, and cook for 3-4 minutes. Add the drained spaghetti, and mix well. Season with salt and pepper. Put the hot buttered spaghetti around the edge of a serving dish, and pour the crab mixture into the center. Garnish with freshly chopped chervil.

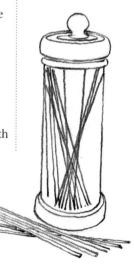

TUNA AND PASTA WITH RED KIDNEY BEANS

This is a substantial salad, suitable for serving as a main course. I sometimes add some diced Edam cheese.

Serves 4-6

INGREDIENTS
8 ounces small pasta shells
1 tablespoon oil
8-ounce can red kidney beans,
  drained and rinsed
4 ounces button mushrooms,
  quartered
7-ounce can tuna, drained and
  flaked
4 scallions, sliced
2 tablespoons freshly chopped
  mixed herbs

Dressing
⅔ cup olive oil
3 tablespoons white wine vinegar
Squeeze of lemon juice
1 tablespoon Dijon mustard
Salt and freshly ground black
  pepper

Cook the pasta shells in boiling salted water with the oil for 10 minutes, or until just tender. Rinse under hot water, and then put into cold water until ready to use. Mix the dressing ingredients together. Drain the pasta shells. Mix the pasta with the beans, mushrooms, tuna, scallions and chopped mixed herbs. Pour the dressing over, and toss the salad well. Chill for up to 1 hour before serving.

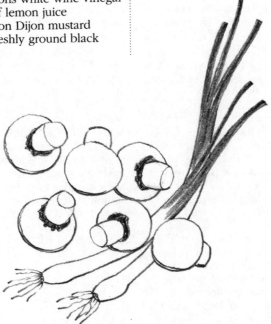

LASAGNE WITH SEAFOOD

This seafood lasagne does not have a sauce topping, so it is covered with foil during baking to prevent it from drying out.

Serves 4-6

4 cups all-purpose flour
4 eggs, lightly beaten
4 tablespoons olive oil
1 pound small clams
1½ pounds live mussels
1 pound shrimp
1 cup dry white wine
2 shallots, chopped
1 onion, finely chopped
2 cloves garlic, chopped
6 tomatoes, skinned, seeded and crushed
2 tablespoons freshly chopped parsley
Salt and freshly ground black pepper
3 tablespoons melted butter
½ cup grated Gruyère cheese
2 teaspoons freshly chopped chervil

In a bowl, mix together the flour and the eggs, using your fingers to form a dough. Shape into a ball, and knead until smooth. Divide the dough into 4, and flatten each piece before passing it through the rollers of a pasta machine. Continue rolling until long, thin strips of pasta are formed. Flour the rollers as necessary during the process. Cut the pasta into small rectangles, and let dry on clean dishcloths for 30 minutes or so. Cook the lasagne, a few sheets at a time, in plenty of boiling, salted water with 1 tablespoon of the olive oil, for 3 minutes. Refresh the lasagne under cold water, then lay it on the dishcloths until required.

Preheat the oven to 400°F. Wash and scrub the clams and mussels. Change the water frequently as you wash. Shell the shrimps and cut in half if they are very large. Pour the wine into a flameproof casserole. Add the shallots and clams and cook, covered, over a high heat until they are open. Remove the clams with a draining spoon; then cook the mussels in the same liquid until they are open. Shell both. Fry the onions and garlic in the remaining olive oil in a skillet. Add the tomatoes and half the chopped parsley. Drain the stock through a strainer lined with cheesecloth. Add the shrimps, clams and mussels, and the cooking liquor, to the pan. Cook over a medium heat for 15-20 minutes. Season to taste.

Brush an ovenproof baking dish with some of the butter. Layer the sheets of lasagne with the seafood mixture. Brush the pasta with butter each time. Finish with a layer of lasagne, and brush it with butter. Top with the cheese and remaining parsley. Cover with foil, and bake for 25 minutes. Remove the foil, then brown the top of the lasagne under a broiler for 5 minutes. Serve garnished with the chopped chervil.

SOUTH SEA NOODLES

A Chinese dish of rice noodles with an attractive and tasty garnish.

Serves 3-4

INGREDIENTS

2 tablespoons Chinese dried
  shrimp, soaked
8 ounces Chinese rice flour
  vermicelli or noodles
4 tablespoons oil
2 onions, sliced
4 rindless bacon slices chopped
2 tablespoons curry powder
Salt
⅔ cup chicken stock

Garnish

2 tablespoons oil
2 cloves garlic, chopped
8 ounces shelled shrimp
1 tablespoon soy sauce
1 tablespoon Hoisin sauce
1 tablespoon pale dry sherry
4 scallions, chopped
2 tablespoons freshly chopped
  parsley

Drain the Chinese shrimp, and chop them. Cook the noodles in boiling, salted water for 3 minutes, then drain and rinse them under cold water. Heat the oil in a wok or heavy-bottomed skillet. Add the onion, bacon and dried shrimp. Stir-fry for 1 minute, then add the curry powder and salt. Fry for 1 minute longer. Add the stock and noodles. Stir over the heat for 2-3 minutes, then transfer to a heated serving platter. For the garnish, heat the oil in a small pan; then add the garlic and shrimp, and stir-fry over a high heat for 1 minute. Add the soy and Hoisin sauces, and sherry. Sprinkle with the scallions and parsley, and pour over the noodles to serve.

SINGAPORE FRIED NOODLES

There is plenty of everything in the busy cosmopolitan port of Shanghai, and the cooking is a rich mixture of many ingredients.

Serves 4

INGREDIENTS

8 ounces egg noodles
3 tablespoons oil
2 eggs, lightly beaten
Salt and freshly ground black pepper
2 cloves garlic, crushed
1 teaspoon chili powder
1 chicken breast, cut into shreds
3 stalks celery, sliced diagonally
2 scallions, sliced
1 red chili, seeded and sliced
1 green chili, seeded and sliced
8 ounces shrimp, shelled and deveined
2 cups bean sprouts

Garnish

Chili flowers (carefully cut the end of the chili into shreds, and soak in cold water until the "flower" opens)

Soak the noodles in boiling water for 8 minutes, or as directed. Drain and let dry on paper towels or a clean dishcloth. Heat a wok or heavy-bottomed skillet, and add 1 tablespoon of the oil. Add the lightly beaten eggs, and salt and pepper to taste. Stir lightly, and cook until set. Remove from the wok or skillet, and cut into thin strips; keep warm. Add the remaining oil to the wok or skillet. When hot, add the garlic and chili powder, and fry for 30 seconds. Add the chicken, celery, scallions and red and green chilis, and stir-fry for 8 minutes, or until chicken has cooked through. Add the noodles, shrimp and bean sprouts, and toss until well mixed and heated through. Serve with the scrambled egg strips on top, and garnish with chili flowers.

FRIED NOODLES WITH SHRIMP

Make certain that the cooked noodles are dry before frying them, so that they do not spatter. This shrimp sauce is slightly sweet and sour, and delicious!

Serves 4

INGREDIENTS

8 ounces fresh noodles
2 tablespoons oil
1 red bell pepper, chopped
1 clove garlic, chopped
20 shrimp, shelled and tails left on
1 drop vinegar
¼ cup orange juice
¼ teaspoon five-spice powder
1 cup fish stock
1 teaspoon cornstarch, combined with a little water
Salt and freshly ground black pepper
Oil for deep-frying

Cook the noodles in boiling, salted water until just tender. Drain and rinse in warm water; then set aside to drain. Heat the oil in a wok or heavy-bottomed skillet, and stir-fry the bell pepper and garlic. Add the shrimp, and cook until crisp; then stir in the vinegar, orange juice, five-spice powder and stock, and cook for 5 minutes. Thicken the sauce by adding the cornstarch mixture and stirring continuously until boiling. Season with salt and pepper.

Heat the oil for deep-frying to 350°F. Add the noodles, and fry them for 2 minutes, then drain on paper towels. Serve the noodles hot with the shrimp sauce.

SHELLFISH IN EGG NOODLE NESTS

A perfect dish to make a big impression on guests! The clams and mussels may be replaced by shrimp or any other shellfish.

Serves 4

INGREDIENTS
4 ounces Chinese egg noodles
24 mussels, washed and
  thoroughly rinsed to remove
  sand
12 small clams, washed and
  thoroughly rinsed to remove
  sand
Scant 1 cup Chinese wine
1 small zucchini
Oil for deep-frying
1 tablespoon oil
1 clove garlic, finely chopped
½ teaspoon finely chopped fresh
  gingerroot
2 leaves bok-choi, shredded
½ tablespoon soy sauce
½ tablespoon oyster sauce
Salt and freshly ground black
  pepper

Cook the egg noodles in boiling, lightly salted water until just tender. Rinse under cold water, and set aside to drain. Cook the mussels and clams with the wine in a large covered saucepan for about 3-5 minutes, until the shells have opened, then remove them from their shells. Thickly peel the zucchini, and slice the peel into thin matchsticks. Discard the flesh and seeds.

Heat the oil in a deep-frying kettle to 350°F. Make the noodle nests by putting a few noodles on the inside of a small frying basket or a metal draining spoon. Clamp the noodles in place with a second basket or draining spoon. Plunge each nest into the hot oil, and cook for 1-2 minutes until golden-brown and crisp. Remove the nest, and drain it on paper towels. Repeat the process with the remaining noodles.

Heat the 1 tablespoon oil in a wok or heavy-bottomed skillet, and stir-fry the garlic, ginger, clams, mussels and bok-choi for 1 minute. Stir in the soy and oyster sauces, and season to taste with salt and pepper. Let the liquid reduce slightly. Divide the mixture evenly between the fried egg noodle nests.

SEAFOOD CHOW MEIN

Chow Mein is a wonderful dish of noodles and vegetables in a rich sauce or gravy. The addition of clams and mussels, or any shellfish, makes it very special.

Serves 4

INGREDIENTS

8 ounces Chinese noodles
½ green bell pepper
½ red bell pepper
1 tablespoon oil
1 garlic clove, chopped
½ teaspoon chopped fresh gingerroot
½ scallion, chopped
1 cup cooked mussels (shelled quantity)
⅓ cup cooked small clams (shelled quantity)
1 tablespoon Chinese wine
2 tablespoons soy sauce
Salt and freshly ground black pepper

Cook the noodles in boiling, salted water until just tender; then rinse them under cold water, and set aside to drain. Cut the bell peppers into thin slices. Heat the oil in a wok or heavy-bottomed skillet, and stir-fry the garlic, gingerroot, bell peppers and scallion for 1 minute. Stir in the mussels, clams, Chinese wine, soy sauce and the cooked noodles. Mix together well, and season with salt and pepper. Serve when heated through completely.

MARINER'S SALAD

A delicious salad with a tangy dressing. Use a selection of your favorite shellfish.

Serves 6

INGREDIENTS

1 pound pasta shells, plain and spinach
4 large scallops, cleaned
8 ounces shelled mussels
⅔ cup lemon juice and water mixed
4 ounces shrimp, shelled and deveined
12 cooked small clams
4 crab sticks, cut into small pieces
4 scallions, chopped
1 tablespoon freshly chopped parsley

Dressing

Grated peel and juice of ½ lemon
1¼ cups mayonnaise
2 teaspoons paprika
⅓ cup sour cream or natural yogurt
Salt and freshly ground black pepper

Cook the pasta for 10 minutes in a large pan of boiling salted water. Drain and rinse under hot water; leave in cold water until ready to use.

Cook the scallops and mussels in the lemon juice and water for about 5 minutes, or until fairly firm. Cut the scallops into 2-3 pieces, depending upon size. Mix the dressing, and drain the pasta thoroughly. Mix all the ingredients together, and coat completely with dressing. Stir carefully, so that the shellfish do not break up. Chill for up to 1 hour before serving.

ITALIAN PASTA PIE

Pasta pies are very filling but very delicious. This one may be scattered with pine nuts before baking, if you wish.

Serves 6-8

INGREDIENTS
1¼ pounds prepared puff pastry dough
1 pound fresh spinach, cooked and drained thoroughly
½ cup ricotta cheese
1 clove garlic, crushed
Salt and freshly ground black pepper
Generous pinch of grated nutmeg
4 ounces pasta shapes, cooked until just tender
½ cup shelled mussels
1 egg, beaten
1 tablespoon freshly chopped basil

To glaze pastry dough
Beaten egg
Grated Parmesan cheese

Preheat the oven to 375°F. Roll out two-thirds of the puff pastry dough quite thinly, and use to line the sides and bottom of a loose-bottomed 7-inch round cake pan. Press the dough carefully into the shape of the pan, avoiding any cracks or splits. Roll out the remaining dough to a round large enough to cover the top of the cake pan generously.

Mix the spinach with the ricotta cheese, garlic, salt and pepper, nutmeg to taste, cooked pasta, mussels, beaten egg and basil. Spoon the filling into the dough-lined pan. Brush the rim of the pastry with some of the beaten egg; then lay the dough lid over the filling, and press the edges together to seal. Trim off any the excess dough, and pinch the edges decoratively. Cut shapes from the dough trimmings to garnish the top of the pie. Glaze with the remaining beaten egg, and sprinkle with grated Parmesan cheese.

Bake for 45 minutes; then cover the pie with a piece of foil, and cook for an additional 20 minutes. Unmold the pie carefully, and serve hot, cut into wedges.

PENNE WITH ANCHOVY SAUCE

This is an unusual sauce but one which makes good use of the favorite Italian ingredient, the anchovy.

Serves 4

INGREDIENTS
6-8 anchovy fillets, drained
2 tablespoons olive oil
14-ounce can chopped tomatoes
3 tablespoons freshly chopped
  parsley
Freshly ground black pepper
10 ounces penne
2 tablespoons melted butter or
  margarine
¼ cup grated Parmesan cheese

Chop the anchovies, and cook them briefly in the oil, stirring until they break up into a paste. Add the chopped tomatoes with the parsley and freshly ground black pepper to taste. Bring to a boil, and simmer, uncovered, for 10 minutes.

Meanwhile, cook the penne in plenty of boiling salted water for 10 minutes, or until *al dente*. Rinse in hot water and drain well; then toss the penne in the melted butter or margarine. Combine the sauce with the pasta, and sprinkle with a little extra chopped parsley. Serve immediately with grated Parmesan cheese.

MACARONI CHEESE WITH ANCHOVIES

I love anchovies and add them to all sorts of dishes – they give an extra dimension to macaroni cheese.

Serves 4

INGREDIENTS
2-ounce can anchovy fillets
8 ounces macaroni
¼ cup butter or margarine
½ cup all-purpose flour
2½ cups milk
½ teaspoon mustard powder
1½ cups grated Gruyère or
  Cheddar cheese
Salt and freshly ground black
  pepper

Drain the anchovies, reserving 4-5 fillets to slice to make a thin lattice over the dish. Chop the rest finely. Cook the macaroni in plenty of boiling salted water for 10 minutes, or until tender but still firm. Rinse in hot water, and drain well.

Meanwhile, melt the butter or margarine in a pan; then stir in the flour, and cook for 1 minute. Remove from the heat, and gradually stir in the milk. Return to the heat, and bring to a boil, stirring continuously. Simmer for 3 minutes, then stir in the mustard, anchovies, and half the cheese. Season with salt and pepper to taste. Stir in the macaroni, and pour into an ovenproof dish. Scatter the remaining cheese over the top, and make a lattice with the remaining anchovies. Brown under a hot broiler, and serve immediately.

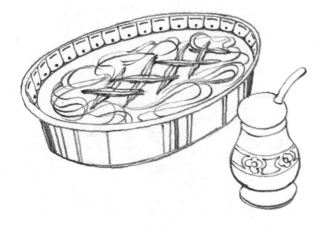

SPAGHETTI ALLA VONGOLE

Vongole is the Italian word for clams, and this is a classic Neapolitan pasta dish.

Serves 4-6

INGREDIENTS
6 tablespoons olive oil
2 pounds live clams
1 pound spaghetti
2 14-ounce cans chopped
   tomatoes
2 cloves garlic, crushed
Salt and freshly ground black
   pepper
2 tablespoons freshly chopped
   parsley

Heat the oil in a large pan. Add the clams, cover the pan, and cook until the shells open, shaking the pan occasionally. Discard the shells, and set the clams aside. Boil the cooking liquor from the clams to reduce by half, then drain through a fine strainer lined with cheesecloth.

Cook the spaghetti in plenty of boiling, salted water until just tender but still firm. Drain and rinse in boiling water, then drain again. Meanwhile, add the tomatoes and garlic to the reduced clam liquor in a pan, and heat through, seasoning to taste. Add the clams, and reheat them slowly. Add the hot spaghetti, and toss until well mixed. Serve, garnished with plenty of freshly chopped parsley.

GARNISHED NOODLES

I think that noodles are far more interesting to serve with a Chinese meal than rice. Nori is a Japanese seaweed, dried in thin sheets.

Serves 4

INGREDIENTS
Sauce
3 tablespoons white wine vinegar
3 tablespoons soy sauce
2 teaspoons sugar
⅔ cup chicken stock or dashi
1 pound Chinese noodles

Garnishes
Cucumber, diced
⅔ cup small shelled shrimp
Celery leaves
2 sheets nori, toasted and
    crumbled or shredded

Combine the vinegar, soy sauce, sugar and stock in a pan, and bring to a boil. Remove from the heat, and keep warm. Cook the noodles in plenty of boiling water for about 5 minutes, until tender. Drain in a colander, and rinse with hot water. Divide the noodles among 4 serving dishes, and arrange the garnishes on top. Pour the sauce over, and serve.

PASTA WITH CHICKEN

Although chicken is one of the most versatile of foods, I have found it to be comparatively, and surprisingly, difficult to assemble an interesting selection of recipes for pasta and chicken. There seem to be so many seafood and meat recipes to choose from, but only a limited number for poultry. Perhaps everyone makes up such recipes as they go along, and never stops to write them down? However, I am certain that the selection which follows will set your taste buds tingling.

176

Chicken, the Perfect Ingredient

Chicken is exceptionally versatile because it has a light flavor of its own which readily marries and mixes with so many other ingredients. Chicken is as happy in a mild creamy sauce with just a flavoring of saffron as it is mixed with olives, anchovies and bell peppers. The ability of chicken to perform as a culinary tonic water, the perfect mixer, is amply illustrated by the number of classic chicken recipes that occur in just about every major cuisine of the world.

Light and Dark Meat for Flavor

Although it is easy and convenient to buy chicken pieces, it is much more expensive than buying a whole bird, and also limits the flavor that you will get from the meat. The whitest meat from a chicken is the breast, which is the most luscious part with the least fat and bone and therefore very little wastage. However, I often find that chicken breasts can be dry and tasteless, and that they are very easy to overcook. My favorite piece from the chicken is the thigh, which is darker meat of a more intense flavor, and it is also considerably cheaper than the breast.

All the recipes that follow require boneless chicken (you wouldn't want great drumsticks mixed into a dish of pasta shapes!), and boneless thighs are available in most supermarkets, although you will pay more for them than the meat on the bone. When I am buying for a recipe which requires boneless chicken meat, I always choose a mixture of breasts and thighs to get a good balance of flavors between the light and dark meat.

Pasta Lunches with Leftover Chicken

Many people find leftover meals to be dull and definitely second-rate, and yet I find that easy lunch dishes made with cooked chicken and pasta offer really satisfying and tasty meals. The cooked chicken is usually reheated in a sauce, so the finished dish can be as flavorsome and inventive as your sauce-making. One of my favorite dishes is the Chicken Bolognese with Nuts; the cashews and walnuts make what might otherwise be a pale imitation of a classic dish into a tasty recipe in its own right. Another of my favorite combinations is a mixture of chicken, pasta and grapes – hot as Chicken Pasta Veronique, or cold as Chicken and Grape Pasta Salad.

Pasta and Chicken the Chinese Way

Pasta and chicken are both very popular in Chinese cookery. The pasta is usually noodles, so it is best to shred the chicken finely to go into such dishes, so that it blends with the noodles instead of dominating them. I like to cook fresh chicken with ginger, or with peaches and scallions, or even with plenty of mixed oriental vegetables in a Chicken Chop Suey. I find that cooked chicken may be made into wonderful lunch dishes by mixing it with a simple stir-fry sauce and noodles, or shrimp and nuts for a more elaborate all-in-one noodle dish.

Chicken-stuffed Tortellini

Tortellini are available dried in most supermarkets and delis, and they are an excellent staple to keep for an emergency. However, the commercial pasta bears almost no resemblance to tortellini made at home, which, although fiddly to fold, are well worth the effort of making. I think that the chicken and spinach filling used in this chapter is one of the nicest that I have tried.

Tortellini are folded to resemble little hats or circles when homemade. The folding of the hats is an art – I usually make the rounds, as directed in the recipe in this chapter! However no tortellini, no matter how delicious their filling or how neatly they are folded, are really enjoyable without a sauce, and the creamy mushroom sauce with the chicken-stuffed tortellini makes a very pleasant change from the more traditional tomato accompaniment.

SPAGHETTI WITH CHICKEN BOLOGNESE AND NUTS

Chicken and nuts. Pasta and nuts. Both are winning combinations. All three ingredients make a very special spaghetti sauce.

Serves 4

INGREDIENTS
Sauce
1 onion, finely chopped
1 clove garlic, finely chopped
2 tablespoons olive oil
Scant 1 cup red wine
2 tablespoons tomato paste
1 tablespoon fresh chopped
  thyme
Salt and freshly ground black
  pepper
1¾ cups finely chopped cooked
  chicken
6 tomatoes, seeded and chopped
1 teaspoon pesto sauce
¼ cup chopped cashew nuts
¼ cup chopped walnuts

12 ounces spaghetti, plain or
  whole wheat

Garnish
Chopped walnuts

Fry the onion and garlic in the olive oil for 3 minutes. Add the red wine, tomato paste, thyme, and salt and pepper to taste. Bring to a boil, and simmer for 10 minutes. Add the chopped chicken, tomatoes, pesto sauce, cashew nuts and walnuts, then simmer the sauce for a few minutes longer.

Meanwhile, cook the spaghetti in boiling, salted water for 8-10 minutes, until just tender. Drain the spaghetti thoroughly. If the sauce is too thick for your liking, thin it down with a little hot stock or water. Pile the cooked spaghetti into a serving dish, and spoon the sauce over the top. Sprinkle with extra chopped walnuts, and serve immediately.

CHICKEN LASAGNE

Lasagne is traditionally made with beef and topped with a white sauce. This lighter version is made with chicken and stock.

Serves 4

INGREDIENTS

3½ cups all-purpose flour
3 eggs, beaten
¼ cup butter
1 onion, chopped
1 clove garlic, chopped
5 cups ground chicken
2 mushrooms, chopped
4 tablespoons white wine
2¼ cups chicken stock
Sprig thyme
1 bay leaf
1 tablespoon tomato paste
Salt and freshly ground black
   pepper
3 tablespoons grated Parmesan
   cheese

Make the dough by mixing together the flour and eggs. Form into a ball, and knead lightly. Coat with a little flour; then wrap and chill for 30 minutes.

Melt half the butter in a skillet, and cook the onion and garlic until lightly browned. Stir in the chicken and mushrooms, and cook for 2 minutes. Add the white wine, and let it reduce.

Stir in 1¼ cups of the chicken stock. Add the thyme, bay leaf and tomato paste, and cook until the liquid has reduced by half. Remove the thyme and bay leaf, and season with salt and pepper.

Preheat the oven to 350°F. Roll the dough out thinly, or pass it through a pasta machine, and cut into equal rectangular strips. Cook for 1 minute in boiling salted water; then rinse under hot water, and set aside to dry slightly on a slightly damp dishcloth. Grease an ovenproof dish with the remaining butter, and lay strips of pasta in the base. Cover each layer of pasta with a layer of the chicken sauce, and continue layering until all the pasta and sauce has been used. Pour the remaining chicken stock into the dish, and sprinkle over the grated Parmesan cheese. Bake until the juices have almost entirely evaporated – about 40 minutes. Serve piping hot from the oven.

MACARONI WITH CREAMY CHICKEN SAUCE

The addition of even a little chopped chicken turns a lunch dish of macaroni cheese into a substantial main course.

Serves 4

INGREDIENTS
1 tablespoon olive oil
4 ounces boneless chicken breast
8 ounces macaroni
¼ cup butter
¼ cup all-purpose flour
2½ cups milk
Salt and freshly ground black
   pepper
1 cup grated or thinly sliced
   mozzarella cheese

Heat the oil in a skillet, and fry the chicken slowly for 10 minutes, or until cooked through. Let cool, then shred the chicken. Cook the macaroni in plenty of boiling salted water for 10 minutes, or until *al dente*; then rinse in hot water, and drain well.

Meanwhile, melt the butter in a pan. Stir in the flour, and cook for 1 minute. Take off the heat, and gradually add the milk, stirring all the time. Bring the sauce to a boil, stirring continuously, and cook for 3 minutes. Add the chicken, macaroni, and salt and pepper to taste, and mix well. Pour the mixture into an flameproof dish, and top with the cheese. Cook under a preheated broiler until golden-brown, then serve immediately.

LASAGNE ROLLS

Roll your own cannelloni!

Serves 4

INGREDIENTS

2 teaspoons vegetable oil
8 sheets lasagne
8 ounces boneless chicken breast
⅔ cup sliced button mushrooms
2 tablespoons butter or
  margarine
¼ cup all-purpose flour
⅔ cup milk
1 cup grated Gruyère or Cheddar
  cheese
Salt and freshly ground black
  pepper

Fill a large saucepan two-thirds full with salted water. Add the oil, and bring to a boil. Add 1 sheet of lasagne, and wait about 2 minutes; then add another sheet. Cook only a few at a time, and when tender, after about 6-7 minutes, remove from the boiling water, and rinse under cold water. Let drain on a dishcloth. Repeat this process until all the lasagne is cooked.

Cut the chicken breast into thin strips. Melt half the butter or margarine in a small skillet, and fry the mushrooms and the chicken for about 10 minutes, until the chicken is just cooked. In a small saucepan, melt the remaining butter. Stir in the flour, and heat slowly for 1 minute. Remove the pan from the heat, and gradually add the milk, stirring well. Return the pan to the heat, and bring to a boil, stirring continuously. Cook for 3 minutes. Pour the sauce over the chicken and mushrooms. Add half the cheese, and mix well; then season to taste.

Lay the sheets of lasagne on a board, and divide the chicken mixture equally between them. Spread the chicken mixture over each lasagne sheet, and roll up lengthwise, like a jelly roll. Put the rolls into an ovenproof dish. Sprinkle with the remaining cheese, and cook under a preheated medium broiler, until the cheese is bubbly and golden-brown.

SHANGHAI NOODLES

*Noodles are more popular in the north of China than in the
rice-growing areas of the south. In Shanghai there is plenty
of everything.*

Serves 4

INGREDIENTS
3 tablespoons oil
4 ounces chicken breasts
1 pound thick Shanghai noodles
  or tagliatelle
2 cups shredded Chinese leaves
4 scallions, thinly sliced
2 tablespoons soy sauce
Freshly ground black pepper
Few drops of sesame oil

Heat the oil in a wok or heavy-bottomed skillet, and add the chicken, cut into thin shreds. Stir-fry for 2-3 minutes. Meanwhile, cook the noodles in boiling salted water until just tender, about 6-8 minutes. Drain in a colander, and rinse under hot water. Toss in the colander to drain, and let dry. Add the shredded Chinese leaves and scallions to the chicken in the wok or skillet, along with the soy sauce, pepper and sesame oil. Cook for about 1 minute, then toss in the cooked noodles. Stir well, and heat through. Serve immediately.

MEXICAN CHICKEN SALAD

Add some chili sauce to the dressing instead of vinegar for a spicier Mexican flavor.

Serves 4

INGREDIENTS

8 ounces small pasta shapes for soup
1½ cups shredded cooked chicken
7-ounce can corn kernels, drained
1 celery stalk, sliced
1 red bell pepper, diced
1 green bell pepper, diced

Dressing
1 tablespoon mayonnaise
2 tablespoons white wine vinegar
Salt and freshly ground black pepper

Cook the pasta in plenty of boiling, salted water until just tender, about 6-8 minutes. Drain well, and let cool. Meanwhile, combine the mayonnaise with the vinegar and salt and pepper to make a dressing. When the pasta is cool, add the chicken, corn, celery and bell peppers. Toss together well, and serve with the dressing.

HERB RAVIOLI WITH CHICKEN STOCK

Homemade ravioli dough is coated with fresh herbs and cooked in a chicken stock flavored with rosemary. This recipe is a soup and pasta dish combined.

Serves 4

INGREDIENTS
1½ cups all-purpose flour
1 egg, beaten
1 bunch chervil, washed and chopped
1 bunch parsley, washed and chopped
4½ cups chicken stock
1 teaspoon dried rosemary
Salt and freshly ground black pepper

Make the dough by mixing together the flour, a good pinch of salt and the egg in a large bowl. Set aside to rest for 30 minutes. Pass the dough through a pasta machine, flouring both sides of the dough as it goes through the rollers to prevent it sticking. Cut the dough into long strips. Alternatively, roll the dough thinly with a rolling pin, and cut into strips. Spread out half of the strips on your counter, and sprinkle over the chervil and parsley. Put the remaining strips on top, and press down well all along the strips with your fingers; then once again run the strips through the rollers of the pasta machine, or reroll with a rolling pin.

Heat the stock and rosemary together in a saucepan until just boiling. Season with salt and pepper. Cut the dough into the desired ravioli shapes. Cook in the boiling stock for 2-4 minutes. Serve very hot in shallow soup plates.

TORTELLINI

Tortellini are like little hats of filled pasta, and are always served with a sauce – I tried them once without, and they were very dry.

Serves 4

INGREDIENTS

Dough
1¼ cups white bread flour
Pinch of salt
1 tablespoon water
1 tablespoon oil
3 eggs, lightly beaten

Filling
2 tablespoons cream cheese
1 cooked chicken breast, finely diced
1 slice ham, shredded
2 spinach leaves, stalks removed, cooked and finely chopped
1 tablespoon grated Parmesan cheese
1 egg, beaten
Salt and freshly ground black pepper

Sauce
1 cup heavy cream
1¼ cups sliced mushrooms
¼ cup grated Parmesan cheese
1 tablespoon freshly chopped parsley
Salt and freshly ground black pepper

Prepare the filling. Beat the cream cheese until soft and smooth; then add the chicken, ham, spinach and Parmesan cheese, and mix well. Add the egg gradually, and salt and pepper to taste. Set aside until required.

To make the pasta dough, sift the flour and salt into a bowl, and make a well in the center. Mix the water, oil and lightly beaten egg together, and pour into the well, working in the flour a little at a time. Continue until the mixture binds together in a ball. Knead on a lightly floured surface for 5 minutes, or until smooth and elastic. Put into a bowl, and cover with a cloth. Let rest for 15 minutes.

Roll the dough out as thinly as possible. Cut into rounds, using a 2-inch cutter, and put half a teaspoonful of filling in the center of each. Fold in half, pressing the edges together firmly. Wrap around a forefinger, and press the ends together.

Cook the tortellini in batches in a large pan of boiling salted water for about 10 minutes until tender, stirring occasionally. Drain.

While the tortellini are cooking, make the sauce. Gently heat the cream in a pan. Add the mushrooms, Parmesan cheese, parsley and salt and pepper to taste. Cook over a low heat for 3 minutes. Toss the sauce together with the tortellini. Serve immediately.

CHINESE CHICKEN WITH PASTA

This is not a classic Chinese dish, but it is delicious!

Serves 2

INGREDIENTS

2 boneless chicken breasts, skinned

Grated peel and juice of half a lime,

Small piece fresh gingerroot, peeled and finely grated

1 clove garlic, crushed

1 tablespoon sesame oil

2 tablespoons light soy sauce

6 ounces tagliatelle

2 tablespoons butter

Salt and freshly ground black pepper

Freshly chopped parsley to garnish

Put the chicken breasts into a small ovenproof casserole. Mix together the peel and juice of the lime, the gingerroot, garlic, sesame oil and soy sauce, and pour the sauce over the chicken. Marinate in a cool place for 4 hours.

Preheat the oven to 375°F. Bake the chicken in the marinade, uncovered, for 30 minutes, turning once. Increase the temperature to 425°F for the final 5 minutes of the cooking time.

While the chicken is baking, cook the pasta in plenty of boiling, salted water until tender but still firm. Drain, then rinse in boiling water and drain again. Melt the butter in the pasta pan. Add the tagliatelle and some freshly ground black pepper, and toss until mixed. Slice the cooked chicken breasts, and add them to the pasta with any remaining sauce. Add extra butter if necessary, and serve immediately garnished with chopped parsley.

CHICKEN PASTA VERONIQUE

Sole is often served in a white wine sauce, garnished with grapes, in a classic French dish called Sole Véronique. The combination of sauce and garnish works just as well with chicken and pasta.

Serves 4

INGREDIENTS
2 tablespoons butter
2 tablespoons olive oil
4 small part-boned chicken breasts, skinned
3-4 scallions, finely sliced
⅔ cup dry white wine
⅔ cup heavy cream
Salt and freshly ground black pepper
12 ounces tagliatelle
Lemon juice
1 cup seeded and halved, black or green grapes, to garnish

Preheat the oven to 375°F. Melt the butter with 1 tablespoon of the olive oil in a skillet. Add the chicken, and cook until well browned on all sides. Remove the chicken from the pan using a draining spoon, and transfer it to an ovenproof dish. Cook the scallions briefly in the fat remaining in the skillet until just soft; then add the wine and cream, and heat slowly. Season with a little salt and pepper. Pour the sauce over the chicken, and bake for 20-30 minutes, until the chicken is cooked through.

Meanwhile, cook the pasta in plenty of boiling, salted water until just tender but still firm, about 10 minutes. Drain, then rinse in boiling water and drain again. Return the pasta to the pan. Add the remaining olive oil and some black pepper, and toss together. Transfer the pasta to a warm serving dish, and arrange the cooked chicken in the center of it. Season the sauce if necessary, adding a squeeze of lemon juice to taste, then spoon the sauce over the chicken. Garnish with the grapes before serving.

189

NOODLES WITH CHICKEN AND SHRIMP

This recipe would serve four as part of a Chinese meal, but would also make a filling lunch dish for two people.

Serves 2-4

INGREDIENTS

8 ounces Chinese noodles
3 tablespoons oil
2 shallots, finely chopped
1 clove garlic, crushed
8 ounces chicken, skinned, boned and cut into small pieces
2 zucchini, cut in strips
3 tablespoons soy sauce
⅓ cup cooked shelled shrimp

Garnish

4 scallions, finely shredded
1 red chili, seeded and finely shredded

Cook the noodles in boiling, salted water until just tender. Drain and rinse under hot water; then toss in a colander to remove excess water. Heat the oil in a wok or heavy-bottomed skillet, and cook the shallots and garlic until softened. Add the chicken, and stir-fry until cooked and the onion and garlic are lightly browned. Add the zucchini and stir-fry about 1-2 minutes. Add the drained noodles, and cook for 2-3 minutes. Add the soy sauce and shrimp. Season with salt and pepper, and cook until thoroughly heated. Serve garnished with the scallions and chili.

STIR-FRIED GLASS NOODLES WITH CHICKEN

This is a typical Thai stir-fry using cellophane noodles to give a finely textured dish.

Serves 4

INGREDIENTS
1 chicken breast, skinned and boned
2 tablespoons oyster sauce
2 tablespoons fish sauce
1 tablespoon soy sauce
1 teaspoon palm sugar
½ large red chili, seeded and chopped
½ teaspoon grated fresh gingerroot
6 ounces cellophane noodles
2 tablespoons oil
2 cloves garlic, crushed
1 red onion, sliced
Cilantro leaves, to garnish

Cut the chicken into thin slices. Combine the oyster sauce, fish sauce, soy, sugar, chili and gingerroot in a shallow dish. Add the chicken, and toss until well coated. Let marinate for 20 minutes.

Soak the noodles in boiling water for 5 minutes, until softened. Drain and set aside. Heat the oil in a wok or heavy-bottomed skillet, and fry the garlic and onion until just softened. Add the chicken and the marinade, and stir-fry for about 10 minutes, or until the chicken is cooked through. Add the noodles to the wok or skillet, and toss over a low heat until heated through. Pile onto a serving dish, and garnish with cilantro leaves.

CHICKEN AND GRAPE
PASTA SALAD

*Chicken and grapes complement each other perfectly. Grapes
are the classic garnish for Coronation Chicken, on which
this recipe is based. It is easiest to use seedless grapes for
this recipe.*

Serves 4-6

INGREDIENTS

12 ounces pasta spirals or bows
1-2 tablespoons olive oil
1 onion, finely chopped
1¾ cups shredded cooked
  chicken
1 red bell pepper, finely chopped
1 cup seeded green grapes
1 cup seeded black grapes
⅔ cup mayonaise
⅔ cup natural yogurt
1-2 teaspoons curry paste
Salt and freshly ground black
  pepper
Freshly chopped cilantro, to
  garnish

Cook the pasta in plenty of
boiling, salted water until tender
but still firm, about 10-12
minutes. Drain, then rinse in cold
water and drain again. Leave
until cold.

Heat the olive oil in a small
skillet. Add the onion, and cook
slowly for 3-4 minutes until
softened. Let cool.

Mix together the chicken and
pepper. Cut the grapes in half
lengthwise if they are large, and
add them to the chicken with the
cold cooked pasta and onion.
Mix together the mayonnaise and
yogurt, and add curry paste to
taste. Season the salad with salt
and pepper; then pour the
dressing over, and toss until the
pasta is well coated. Chill until
required, and garnish with
cilantro just before serving.

PASTA WITH MEAT

Without doubt the vast majority of pasta recipes, and certainly most of the classic recipes, are Italian in origin. That is, of course, excepting those for noodles and vermicelli that are Chinese! So, many of the recipes that are featured in this chapter on pasta and meat include the most popular ingredients in the Italian cuisine.

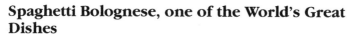

Spaghetti Bolognese, one of the World's Great Dishes

Spaghetti Bolognese derives its name from the town of Bologna in the Emilia-Romagna region of northern Italy. Referred to as *Bologna la grassa*, Bologna the fat, this city is the culinary capital of northern Italy, producing delicious and very rich food from the wealth of top-quality ingredients that are produced in the surrounding region. These included Parma ham, Parmesan cheese, and balsamic vinegar.

A Bolognese sauce may be made with ground beef only, or with a mixture of ground beef and pork and some chopped chicken livers. The latter is the more traditional style of the gastronomes of Bologna, as it produces a richer sauce of more complex flavors than a straight beef mixture. The richest of sauces may have a little brandy added to the browned meats, but it is far more usual to add some red wine, and to reduce that for a strong flavor in the sauce, if some alcohol is required. I always like to add a few mushrooms to a Bolognese – others add peas, carrots or even broccoli flowerets.

Spaghetti Bolognese must be one of the most popular dishes in the world, which, in a sense, is responsible for the move away from the most traditional meat sauce with chicken livers to any one of the numerous recipes that exist, bearing the classic name of Bolognese. When I have my Very Serious Cook's hat on, I get upset about this, and feel that it leads to a watering down of an important culinary heritage. However, for most of the time, when I am trying to encourage people to enjoy cooking and eating, I feel that as long as there is love in the preparation of a meal and enjoyment in the eating, the actual name of the dish does not really matter.

Game Sauces for Pasta

The Italians are great meat-eaters, and, alongside beef, veal, pork and chicken, they also enjoy a wide variety of game. Hare and rabbit are both popular, so it is no surprise to find recipes in this chapter for a hare sauce and a ravioli stuffed with rabbit. I feel that this is good, as such dishes provide different and imaginative ways of serving simple country food. I, for one, would far rather eat a hare sauce on pasta than hare jugged with its blood. It is a great shame that recipes such as the latter can put us off the basic ingredient, and prevent us from trying other, delicious dishes.

Sweet and Flavorsome Bacon

So often bacon is just regarded as a breakfast food, and a seasoning to fry with vegetables at the start of a complicated meat dish. Good bacon is not always easy to find – much of that which is pre-packed seems to be very wet and watery, and to spatter in the skillet, and never go crisp. Perhaps that limits its use to a *mirepoix*, a mixture of finely diced vegetables and bacon sweated in butter. However, get hold of a good piece of well cured, dry bacon, and you have the basis of some wonderful pasta dishes.

What is the difference between bacon and ham? Well, bacon is taken from the back or side of a pig, and hams are produced mainly from the back legs, and are cured much more slowly than bacon. The shoulder or front leg is also used to produce ham, but this is of a lesser quality than the prime joints from the back leg.

Bacon is usually cured in brine, although a better flavor is produced when it is dry-cured. A very mild cure is known as tendersweet, but it produces a very mild bacon. The bacon may then be smoked, adding extra flavor and color to the meat. Bacon that has not been smoked is sometimes referred to as *green*, an unfortunate term as it makes one think of food that has gone off! However, for cooking I certainly prefer to use green bacon as I like the true bacon flavor without the smoke.

Carbonara is probably the most famous pasta sauce with bacon. In the recipe for Tagliatelli Carbonara in this chapter a little paprika is added to the bacon during cooking – I sometimes omit the paprika, and add a clove (or two) of crushed garlic.

PASTA AL FORNO

"Al forno" means baked in the oven, so this is oven-baked pasta.

Serves 4

INGREDIENTS
8 ounces macaroni
¼ cup butter or margarine
½ cup grated Parmesan cheese
Pinch of grated nutmeg
Salt and freshly ground black
  pepper
2 eggs, beaten
1 onion, chopped
1 clove garlic, crushed
4 cups ground beef
2 tablespoons tomato paste
6 tablespoons beef stock
2 tablespoons freshly chopped
  parsley
4 tablespoons red wine
2 tablespoons all-purpose plain
  flour
⅔ cup milk

Preheat the oven to 375°F. Cook the macaroni in plenty of boiling salted water for 10 minutes, or until tender but still firm. Rinse under hot water, and drain. Put one-third of the butter or margarine in the pan, and return the macaroni to it. Add half the cheese, nutmeg, and salt and pepper to taste, and let cool. Mix in half the beaten egg, and set aside until required.

Melt half the remaining butter or margarine in a pan, and fry the onion and garlic slowly until the onion is soft. Increase the heat; then add the meat, and fry until browned. Add the tomato paste, stock, parsley and wine, and season with salt and pepper. Simmer for 20 minutes. Melt the remaining butter or margarine in a small pan. Stir in the flour, and cook for 30 seconds; then remove from the heat, and gradually stir in the milk. Bring to a boil, stirring continuously, until the sauce thickens. Beat in the remaining egg, and season to taste. Spoon half the macaroni into a serving dish, and cover with the meat sauce. Add another layer of macaroni. Add the white sauce, and top with remaining cheese. Bake for 30 minutes, until golden-brown. Serve immediately.

TAGLIATELLE WITH BACON AND TOMATO SAUCE

Serves 4

INGREDIENTS
1 tablespoon olive oil
1 onion, finely chopped
6 rindless bacon slices cut into
strips
2 tablespoons freshly chopped
parsley
2 tablespoons freshly chopped
basil
14-ounces can chopped tomatoes
Salt and freshly ground black
pepper
10 ounces tagliatelle
½ cup grated pecorino cheese

Heat the oil in a large pan. Add the onion and bacon, and cook slowly until the onion is soft, but not browned. Add the parsley, basil and tomatoes, and simmer slowly for 5 minutes, stirring occasionally. Season to taste with salt and pepper.

Meanwhile, cook the tagliatelle in a large pan of boiling salted water. Cook for about 10 minutes, until *al dente*. Drain and return the pasta to the pan. Add the sauce, and toss thoroughly. Serve with grated pecorino cheese.

FRIED NOODLES WITH PORK AND VEGETABLES

The boiled noodles need to be dried thoroughly before frying to prevent any spatter. Taro is a potato-like vegetable, very similar to edo, which are available in some large supermarkets.

Serves 4

INGREDIENTS

12 ounces fresh noodles
1 taro or edo
1 tablespoon oil
1 clove garlic, chopped
1 carrot, cut into sticks
8 ounces Chinese leaves, thinly sliced
8 ounces cooked pork meat, thinly sliced
1 tablespoon soy sauce
1¼ cups chicken stock
Salt and freshly ground black pepper
Oil for deep-frying
1 teaspoon cornstarch, combined with a little water

Cook the noodles in boiling, salted water. Rinse in warm water, and set aside to drain. Prepare the taro or edo by first slicing off the end, then peeling with a potato peeler. Lastly, using the potato peeler, cut the taro into thin slices. Heat the oil in a wok or heavy-bottomed skillet, and stir-fry the taro or edo, garlic, carrot and Chinese leaves. Add the pork, soy sauce, stock, and salt and pepper. Cook over a low heat for 5 minutes, shaking the wok or skillet frequently.

Heat the oil for deep-frying to 350°F, and fry the noodles a few at a time. Drain the noodles on paper towels. Divide the noodles equally between four small plates. Remove the vegetables and pork mixture from the wok or skillet with a draining spoon, and serve over the noodles. Stir the cornstarch into the remaining sauce in the wok or skillet, and stir until the sauce boils and thickens. Pour some over each plate of noodles, and serve immediately.

PORK WRAPPED IN NOODLES

This recipe is not as fiddly as it sounds! The meatballs are only mildly spiced, and should be served with a hot chili dipping sauce.

Serves 4

INGREDIENTS
2 cups ground pork
1 teaspoon ground coriander
1 tablespoon fish sauce
1 small egg, beaten
3 ounces rice noodles
  (vermicelli)
Oil for deep-frying
Whole chilis, to garnish

Mix together the pork, coriander and fish sauce, then add enough egg to bind. Roll the mixture into small balls, and chill for 30 minutes. Cover the noodles with warm water, and soak for about 10 minutes to soften. Drain the noodles, and wrap several strands around each pork ball. Heat the oil in a wok or heavy-bottomed skillet, and deep-fry a few of the meatballs at a time for 3-4 minutes, or until crisp and golden. Drain on paper towels, and garnish with whole chilis.

CHAING MAI NOODLES

The coconut milk used in this recipe gives an unusual but typically Thai flavor to this noodle dish.

Serves 4-6

INGREDIENTS

2 tablespoons oil
2 cloves garlic, crushed
4 shallots, chopped
1 tablespoon red curry paste
½ teaspoon ground turmeric
Pinch of ground cumin
Pinch of ground coriander
1¼ cups coconut milk
8 ounces sirloin steak, thinly
   sliced
5 tablespoons fish sauce
¼ cup palm sugar
1 tablespoon soy sauce
2 tablespoons lime juice
1 tablespoon freshly chopped
   garlic chives
1 pound fresh egg noodles

Heat the oil in a wok or heavy-bottomed skillet, and fry the garlic and shallots until softened. Stir in the curry paste, turmeric, cumin and coriander. Stir-fry for 1 minute. Add the coconut milk, and bring to a boil. Reduce the heat, and add the beef. Simmer for 15-20 minutes, or until the beef is cooked. Stir in the fish sauce, sugar, soy, lime juice and garlic chives. Meanwhile, cook the egg noodles in boiling water for 1 minute. Drain the noodles, and arrange on a serving dish. Spoon the beef on top, and serve.

PENNE WITH HAM AND ASPARAGUS

Penne are pasta tubes, cut diagonally in the shape of a quill. Penne actually means quill.

Serves 4

INGREDIENTS
12 ounces fresh asparagus
4 ounces cooked ham
2 tablespoons butter or margarine
2¼ cups heavy cream
Salt and freshly ground black pepper
8 ounces penne
Grated Parmesan cheese

Using a swivel vegetable peeler, scrape the sides of the asparagus stalks, starting about 2 inches from the tips. Cut off the ends of the stalks about 1 inch from the bottom. Cut the ham into strips about ½ inch thick. Bring a sauté pan or skillet of water to a boil, adding a pinch of salt. Move the pan so it is half on and half off the direct heat. Add the asparagus stalks so that the tips are off the heat. Cover the pan, and return it to a boil. Cook the asparagus stalks for about 2 minutes. Drain and let cool. Cut the asparagus into 2-inch lengths, leaving the tips whole.

Melt the butter or margarine in the sauté pan or skillet, and add the asparagus and ham. Cook briefly to evaporate any liquid, then add the cream. Bring to a boil, and cook for about 5 minutes to thicken the cream. Season to taste. Meanwhile, cook the pasta in boiling salted water for about 10-12 minutes. Drain the pasta, and rinse under hot water. Toss in a colander to drain, then mix with the sauce. Serve with grated Parmesan cheese, if wished.

LAMB WITH PASTA AND TOMATOES

This delicious dish is a classic Greek way of serving lamb, with pasta to make the meat go farther.

Serves 6-8

INGREDIENTS
1 lamb shoulder or leg, about 3 pounds in weight
2 cloves garlic, cut into thin slivers
4 tablespoons olive oil
8 ounces pasta shells, spirals or other shapes
2½ cups lamb or beef stock or water
1 pound fresh tomatoes or 14-ounce can tomatoes
1 tablespoon freshly chopped oregano
Salt and freshly ground black pepper
Grated Parmesan cheese

Preheat the oven to 400°F. Cut slits at about 2-inch intervals all over the lamb. Insert small slivers of garlic into each slit. Put the lamb into a large roasting pan and rub the surface with the olive oil. Roast for about 60 minutes, basting occasionally.

Meanwhile, parboil the pasta for about 5 minutes in boiling salted water, and rinse in hot water. Turn the meat over in the roasting pan and add the stock or water, pasta and additional seasoning. Mix the tomatoes with the oregano, and salt and pepper, and pour over the lamb. Stir well. Cook for an additional 20-30 minutes, stirring the pasta occasionally to ensure even cooking. When the pasta is completely cooked, turn the lamb over again, and sprinkle with some cheese before carving and serving with the pasta.

ITALIAN PASTA SALAD

Serve this salad with sliced tomatoes and Italian olive oil bread.

Serves 4-6

INGREDIENTS

1 pound pasta shapes
¾ cup frozen peas
8 ounces assorted Italiana meats, cut in strips: salami, mortadella, prosciutto, coppa, bresaola
4 ounces provolone or fontina cheese, cut in strips
15 black olives, halved and pitted
4 tablespoons small capers
1 small red onion or 2 shallots, chopped
6 ounces oyster mushrooms, stems trimmed and sliced

Dressing

3 tablespoons white wine vinegar
⅔ cup olive oil
½ clove garlic, ground
1 teaspoon fennel seeds, crushed
1 tablespoon freshly chopped parsley
1 tablespoon freshly chopped basil
1 tablespoon mustard
Salt and freshly ground black pepper

Cook the pasta in a large pan of boiling salted water for about 10 minutes, or until just tender. Add the frozen peas during the last 3 minutes of cooking time. Drain the pasta and peas, and rinse under hot water. Leave in cold water until ready to use.

Mix the dressing ingredients together. Drain the pasta and peas, and mix with the Italian meats and cheeses, olives, capers, chopped onion or shallot and sliced mushrooms. Pour the dressing over the salad, and toss all the ingredients together. Do not overmix. Let the salad chill for up to 1 hour before serving.

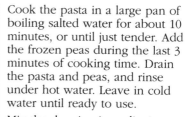

TORTELLINI WITH MUSHROOMS AND BACON

Fresh tortellini are quite time-consuming to prepare, but the dried or fresh ones available in supermarkets make a good, quick lunch dish when served in a tasty sauce.

Serves 4

INGREDIENTS
1 cup chopped, rindless bacon
1 small onion, chopped
3 teaspoons cornstarch
⅔ cup milk
8 ounces small button mushrooms
2 teaspoons ground coriander
1¼ cups light cream
Salt and freshly ground black pepper
8 ounces prepared tortellini, dried or fresh
Freshly chopped cilantro leaves

Cook the bacon slowly until the fat runs out. Add the onions, and cook for 5 minutes until soft. Add the cornstarch, and cook for 2 minutes; then gradually add the milk and bring slowly to a boil. Add the mushrooms, and cook for 2 minutes longer. Add the ground coriander and cream, and heat through. Season to taste. Cook the tortellini as directed on the package, then fold them into the sauce. Serve garnished with fresh cilantro.

LAYERED PASTA SALAD

This layered salad may be prepared the day before it is required – but I prefer to make such dishes on the day.

Serves 4

INGREDIENTS
4 ounces pasta tubes or spirals
1½ cups frozen peas
1 red onion, thinly sliced
4 radishes, sliced
Crisp lettuce leaves
8 ounces cooked ham, cut into strips
1½ cups diced Cheddar cheese
Freshly chopped parsley to garnish

Dressing
⅔ cup mayonnaise
⅔ cup sour cream
1 tablespoon Dijon or whole grain mustard

Cook the pasta in plenty of boiling, salted water until tender. Drain and rinse in cold water; then let cool. Cook the frozen peas, drain and cool. Mix together the onion and radishes.

Put the torn lettuce leaves into a large glass bowl. Follow with a layer of the ham, then the cheese, half the onion mixture, the pasta, another layer of onion mix, and lastly the peas. Combine the dressing ingredients, and spread over the salad. Garnish with chopped parsley.

RABBIT RAVIOLI WITH TARRAGON

This is a well-flavored, country dish. Chicken may be used instead of the rabbit, if preferred.

Serves 4

INGREDIENTS
2½ cups all-purpose flour
4 eggs, lightly beaten
½ leek
1 onion
1 carrot
3 rabbit thigh portions
2 tablespoons olive oil
5 sprigs tarragon
Bouquet garni
Salt and freshly ground black
  pepper
4 tablespoons heavy cream

Put the flour into a bowl, and add 3 of the eggs. Mix with your fingers to make a dough, and form it into a ball. Knead until smooth, then set aside to rest. Dice the leek, onion and carrot. Fry the rabbit in the oil until lightly browned. Remove the tarragon leaves from 3 sprigs; reserve the stalks for the stock, and chop the leaves. Add the onion, carrot, leek, tarragon stalks and bouquet garni to the rabbit. Cook for 2 minutes, then add 3 cups of water. Cook, covered, over a low heat for 1½ hours. Remove the rabbit portions from the pan, and take the meat off the bones. Chop it very finely, and mix with three-quarters of the tarragon leaves. Season with salt and pepper. Drain the stock through a fine strainer, and set aside.

Divide the dough into smaller, flat rounds, and pass them through a pasta machine to form thin pasta strips. Cut the pasta into equal rectangles to make ravioli. Mix 2 tablespoons of the rabbit stock into the meat and tarragon, and put about 1 teaspoonful of the mixture in the center of each piece of pasta. Brush the edges of the dough with the remaining beaten egg, and fold over the filling to make the ravioli. Pinch the edges together with your fingers; then using a cooky cutter, shape into rounds. Cook the ravioli for 5 minutes in plenty of salted boiling water with the last sprig of tarragon. Drain with a draining spoon.

Reduce 2 cups of the rabbit stock by half. Add the cream. Season to taste, and heat through. Serve the ravioli and cream sauce in soup plates. Garnish with the remaining chopped tarragon.

SICILIAN CANNELLONI

Cannelloni should be cooked in quite a small dish, so that the tops become crisp, but the rest of the filled pasta remains soft and moist.

Serves 4

INGREDIENTS
16 cannelloni shells
¼ cup butter
1 shallot, chopped
4 mushrooms, chopped
2 slices ham, chopped
2½ cups ground braising beef
Salt and freshly ground black pepper
Butter for greasing
10 thin slices mozzarella cheese
½ cups chicken stock

Preheat the oven to 400°F. Cook the cannelloni in salted, boiling water for 5 minutes. Rinse in hot water, then set aside to drain. Melt the butter in a saucepan or flameproof casserole, and cook the shallot, mushrooms, ham and beef for about 10 minutes. Season with salt and pepper, and set aside to cool. When cooled, fill the cannelloni with the mixture, and put into a lightly greased, ovenproof dish. Lay the slices of mozzarella over the cannelloni, and pour in the chicken stock.

Bake the cannelloni for 15-25 minutes until thoroughly heated with a crisp and golden top. Serve piping hot.

MEAT RAVIOLI WITH RED BELL PEPPER SAUCE

Red bell peppers are used to color the pasta and flavor the sauce for this innovative and unusual dish.

Serves 4

INGREDIENTS
2 red bell peppers
1¾ cups all-purpose flour
2 eggs, lightly beaten
1½ cups ground beef
1 tablespoon freshly chopped
　parsley
½ onion, chopped
Salt and freshly ground black
　pepper
½ cup light cream
⅓ cup butter

Put the red bell peppers into a food processor, and blend until liquid. Transfer to a small bowl, and set aside until the pulp rises to the surface. This takes about 30 minutes.

To make the dough, put the flour into a bowl, and add 1 egg and 3 tablespoons of the red bell pepper pulp (not the juice). Mix thoroughly, and form into a ball. Knead lightly, then set the dough aside for 30 minutes. Mix together the meat, parsley and onion, and season with salt and pepper. Roll the dough out very thinly, using a pasta machine if available, and cut into small squares. Put a little stuffing on half of the cut squares. Beat the remaining egg, and brush the edges of the dough with the egg. Cover with another square of dough, and seal the edges by pinching together with your fingers.

Bring a large saucepan of salted water to a boil, and cook the ravioli for about 3 minutes – longer if you prefer your pasta well cooked. While the ravioli are cooking, prepare the sauce by heating the cream with ½ cup of the red bell pepper pulp. Bring to a boil, and then whisk in the butter. Drain the ravioli. Serve the pasta with the hot cream sauce poured over.

COUNTRYSIDE SAUCE WITH FRESH PASTA

This sauce, is quick and easy to prepare from staple ingredients.

Serves 4

INGREDIENTS
11 ounces pasta
1 tablespoon olive oil
1 onion, sliced
2 slices ham, cut into small
  pieces
6 freshly chopped basil leaves
Tomato, seeded and chopped
Salt and freshly ground black
  pepper
¼ cup butter
2 tablespoons grated Parmesan
  cheese

Cook the pasta in boiling salted water until tender but still firm. Rinse under hot water, and set aside to drain. Heat the olive oil in a skillet, and cook the onion, ham, basil and tomato slowly for about 20 minutes. Season with salt and pepper. Melt the butter in a saucepan, and add the pasta, stirring well. Stir in the sauce, and serve when the pasta is hot, topped with the grated Parmesan.

WHOLE WHEAT SPAGHETTI WITH PEAS AND BACON

Peas and bacon in plenty of butter make a simple but tasty flavoring for this pasta.

Serves 4

INGREDIENTS
10 ounces whole wheat spaghetti
2 cups shelled peas
1 teaspoon sugar
⅓ cup butter or margarine
¾ cup diced, rindless bacon
Salt and freshly ground black pepper
Freshly chopped parsley, to garnish (optional)

Cook the spaghetti in plenty of boiling salted water for 10 minutes, or until tender but still firm. Meanwhile, cook the peas in boiling water with a pinch of salt and the sugar. Melt the butter in a pan, and fry the bacon. When crisp, add the drained peas, and salt and pepper to taste, then pour over the spaghetti. Toss and serve immediately, garnished with chopped parsley if wished.

BRASCIOLE WITH TAGLIATELLE

This is an elegant dish for a dinner party – the veal rolls may be prepared ahead, and chilled until needed.

Serves 4

INGREDIENTS
4 veal steaks
4 thin slices ham
¼ cup grated Parmesan cheese
Salt and freshly ground black
  pepper
2 tablespoons butter or
  margarine
14-ounce can tomatoes, strained,
  or passata (strained tomato
  purée)
8 ounces tagliatelle

Bat the veal steaks thinly between two sheets of dampened baking parchment. Lay a slice of ham on the top of each steak, and sprinkle each with a tablespoon of the Parmesan cheese and some freshly ground black pepper. Roll up from a short side, like a jelly roll, tucking the slices in to form neat packages. Tie gently with string at each end and in the middle. Melt the butter or margarine in a pan, and add the veal rolls. Cook slowly until lightly browned all over. Add the strained tomatoes. Cover the pan, and cook for 15 minutes. Meanwhile, cook the tagliatelle in plenty of boiling salted water for 10 minutes, or until tender but still firm. Rinse in hot water and drain.

Remove the string, and cut the veal rolls into 1-inch slices. Toss the tagliatelle together with the tomato sauce, and top with the veal and grated Parmesan cheese. Serve immediately.

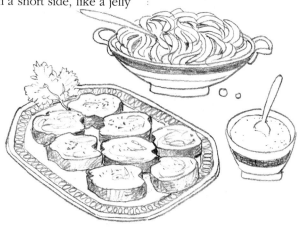

HARE SAUCE WITH WHOLE-WHEAT SPAGHETTI

This dish has a strong, gamy flavor, and is a good way of using up a small amount of hare meat.

Serves 4

INGREDIENTS

2 tablespoons olive oil
8 ounces boneless hare, cut into small pieces
2 onions, sliced
¾ cup diced, rindless bacon
1 clove garlic, crushed
1 teaspoon freshly chopped oregano
2 tablespoons all-purpose flour
⅔ cup red wine
Salt and freshly ground black pepper
10 ounces whole-wheat spaghetti

Heat the oil in a heavy pan. Lightly brown the hare pieces, then remove them with a draining spoon and set aside. Add the onions, bacon, garlic and oregano to the oil, and fry until lightly colored. Take the pan off the heat, and stir in the flour. Return the pan to the heat, and cook for 2 minutes. Remove from the heat again, and gradually add the wine. Bring to a boil, stirring continuously. Add the hare; cover the pan, and simmer slowly for about 1 hour, until the hare is tender. Add salt and pepper to taste. When the sauce is ready, cook the spaghetti in plenty of boiling salted water for about 10 minutes, or until tender but still firm. Rinse in hot water, and drain. Serve the hare sauce on a bed of the freshly cooked pasta.

SPAGHETTI WITH EGG, BACON AND MUSHROOM

Spaghetti, eggs and bacon make a classic combination of ingredients, and the mushrooms add extra flavor to the dish.

Serves 4

INGREDIENTS
¼ cup butter or margarine
2½ cups sliced mushrooms
¾ cup diced, rindless bacon
10 ounces spaghetti
Salt and freshly ground black pepper
2 eggs, hard-cooked and finely chopped
1 tablespoon freshly chopped parsley
1½ cups grated Parmesan cheese

Melt half the butter or margarine in a skillet. Add the mushrooms and bacon, and cook for 10 minutes over a medium heat, until the bacon is crisp. Meanwhile, cook the spaghetti in plenty of boiling salted water until tender but still firm – about 10 minutes. Drain and return to the pan. Add the remaining butter or margarine, salt and plenty of freshly ground black pepper, and the mushrooms and bacon. Toss together. Serve topped with the hard-cooked eggs and parsley. Pass the grated Parmesan cheese separately.

PASTA SPIRALS WITH KIDNEYS IN MARSALA SAUCE

Kidneys are one of my favorite foods – I cook them with plenty of black pepper and serve them on a bed of pasta.

Serves 4

INGREDIENTS
8 ounces lamb kidneys
Salt and freshly ground black
  pepper
1 tablespoon all-purpose flour
¼ cup butter or margarine
1 small onion, finely chopped
1 clove garlic crushed
⅔ cup diced, rindless bacon
1¼ cups sliced button
  mushrooms
⅓ cup Marsala, or dry white
  wine
10 ounces pasta spirals

Remove the skin, fat and hard core from the kidneys. Cut in half lengthwise. Add salt and pepper to the flour, and mix well; then coat the kidneys in the seasoned flour.

Melt the butter or margarine in a pan. Add the onion and garlic, and cook until soft but not browned. Add the kidneys, and brown all over. Add the bacon and mushrooms, and cook, stirring frequently, for 3 minutes; then add the Marsala, and bring to a boil. Simmer slowly for 15 minutes, or until the kidneys are tender. Adjust the seasoning to taste.

Meanwhile, cook the pasta spirals in plenty of boiling salted water for 10 minutes, or until tender but still firm. Rinse in hot water, and drain well. Serve the kidneys on a bed of the freshly cooked pasta.

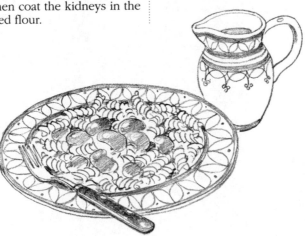

SPAGHETTI WITH SWEETBREAD CARBONARA

Sweetbreads are used instead of bacon for this variation of a popular classic. Stir the eggs into the spaghetti over a low heat until they just start to thicken, if necessary.

Serves 4

INGREDIENTS

1 onion, chopped
3 tablespoons olive oil
12 ounces whole wheat spaghetti
8 ounces calves' sweetbreads, blanched, skinned and chopped
6 tablespoons dry white wine
4 eggs, lightly beaten
½ cup grated Parmesan cheese
2 tablespoons freshly chopped basil
1 clove garlic, crushed
Salt and freshly ground black pepper
Fresh basil, to garnish

Fry the onion slowly in the olive oil for 5 minutes. Meanwhile, cook the spaghetti in a large pan of boiling, salted water for about 10 minutes, until just tender. Add the chopped sweetbreads to the onion, and fry slowly for 4 minutes; then add the white wine, and cook briskly until it has almost evaporated. Beat the eggs with the Parmesan cheese, basil, garlic, and salt and pepper. Drain the spaghetti thoroughly; immediately stir in the beaten egg mixture and the sweetbreads so that the heat from the spaghetti cooks the eggs. Garnish with basil, and serve immediately.

TAGLIATELLE CARBONARA

This dish is often made with spaghetti, but I prefer to use tagliatelle.

Serves 2

INGREDIENTS
1 tablespoon olive oil
¾ cup chopped, rindless bacon
Pinch of paprika
4 tablespoons light cream
2 eggs, lightly beaten
¼ cup grated Parmesan cheese
10 ounces tagliatelle
2 tablespoons butter or
   margarine
Salt and freshly ground black
   pepper

Heat the oil in a skillet. Add the bacon, and cook over a medium heat until browned. Add the paprika, and cook for 1 minute; then add the cream, and stir. Beat together the eggs and grated cheese.

Meanwhile, cook the tagliatelle in plenty of boiling salted water for 10 minutes, or until tender but still firm. Drain; then return to the pan with the butter or margarine and black pepper, and toss. Add the bacon mixture and the egg mixture, and toss together over a low heat until the egg is just setting. Add salt to taste. Serve immediately.

PENNE WITH SPICY CHILI SAUCE

Penne are slightly thicker than macaroni – I like them because more sauce gets trapped inside the tubes!

Serves 4-6

INGREDIENTS
14-ounce can plum tomatoes
1 tablespoon olive oil
2 cloves garlic, crushed
1 onion, chopped
4 bacon slices, chopped
2 red chilis, seeded and chopped
2 scallions, chopped
½ cup grated pecorino or
  Parmesan cheese
1 pound penne or macaroni
Salt and freshly ground black
  pepper

Chop the tomatoes, and strain them to remove the seeds. Alternatively, use a can of chopped tomatoes. Heat the oil in a skillet, and fry the garlic, onion and bacon slowly for 6-8 minutes. Add the strained tomatoes, chilis, scallions and half the cheese. Simmer slowly for 20 minutes, then season to taste.

Cook the penne or macaroni in boiling salted water for 10-15 minutes, or until tender. Rinse under hot water, and drain well. Put the cooked penne into a warm serving dish with half the sauce, and toss them together to coat the pasta. Pour the remaining sauce over the top, and sprinkle with the remaining cheese before serving.

MEE GORENG

*I love Indonesian food, which is spicy and hot. This dish of
mixed noodles is quick to prepare, but have everything
chopped before you start cooking. Use chili sauce if chili
paste is not available.*

Serves 4

INGREDIENTS
8 ounces fine egg noodles
4 tablespoons peanut oil
1 onion, finely chopped
2 cloves garlic, crushed
1 green chili, seeded and finely
  sliced
1 teaspoon chili paste
4 ounces pork tenderloin, finely
  sliced
2 celery stalks, sliced
¼ small cabbage, finely shredded
1 tablespoon light soy sauce
¾ cup shelled and deveined,
  cooked shrimp
Salt and freshly ground black
  pepper

Soak the noodles in hot water for
8 minutes, until they are soft.
Rinse in cold water, and drain
thoroughly in a colander.

Heat the oil in a wok or heavy-
bottomed skillet, and stir-fry the
onion, garlic and chili until the
onion is soft and just golden-
brown. Add the chili paste, and
stir well; then add the pork,
celery and cabbage to the fried
onions, and stir-fry for about 3
minutes, or until the pork is
cooked through. Season to taste.
Stir in the soy sauce, noodles and
shrimp, tossing the mixture
together and heating through
before serving.

MACARONI AU GRATIN

This is a typical Mediterranean dish, and a very good way of turning just a little meat into a satisfying meal for four.

Serves 4

INGREDIENTS
1 pound macaroni
¼ cup butter
Salt and freshly ground black
  pepper
1 cup grated Parmesan cheese
2 cups ground lamb
3 tablespoons bread crumbs

Preheat the oven to 400°F. Cook the macaroni in boiling, salted water. Drain and rinse; then set aside to drain. Melt the butter, and fry the macaroni rapidly, seasoning it with salt and pepper. Put a layer of macaroni in the bottom of a greased ovenproof dish, and then a layer of cheese. Sprinkle the meat over the cheese, and then cover the meat with another layer of macaroni. Sprinkle over another layer of cheese, and then all the bread crumbs. Bake for 20-30 minutes, and serve immediately.

PHARAOH'S WHEEL
NOODLES

This recipe is based on a traditional Jewish dish, said to symbolize the Jews' crossing of the Red Sea. I prefer to use tomato sauce, rather than the meat sauce, and let the salami flavor the dish.

Serves 6

INGREDIENTS
8 ounces egg noodles, cooked until *al dente*
2 cups Italian meat sauce or tomato sauce
8 ounces salami, thinly sliced
⅓ cup raisins
½ cup pine nuts

Preheat the oven to 400°F. Grease a large ovenproof round, glass baking dish. Arrange a layer of cooked noodles in the dish, then pour some of the sauce over them. Arrange a ring of salami around the edge of the dish, and sprinkle some raisins and pine nuts in the center. Add another layer of pasta, and repeat the sauce, salami, raisins and pine nuts. Continue layering until all the ingredients are used up, finishing with a layer of salami. Bake for 20 minutes, or until heated through. Serve immediately.

SPAGHETTI WITH TOMATO, SALAMI AND GREEN OLIVES

Salami is usually eaten cold, but it makes a really great addition to hot pasta dishes.

Serves 3-4

INGREDIENTS
14-ounce can plum tomatoes or passata
2 teaspoons freshly chopped oregano
1 cup sliced and shredded salami
1¾ cups pitted and chopped green olives
Salt and freshly ground black pepper
10 ounces spaghetti
2 tablespoons olive oil
1 clove garlic, crushed
½ cup grated pecorino cheese

Paste the tomatoes in a blender or food processor, then press through a strainer into a saucepan. Alternatively, use passata. Add the oregano, salami and olives, and heat slowly. Add salt and pepper to taste.

Meanwhile, cook the spaghetti in plenty of boiling, salted water for 10 minutes, or until tender but still firm. Drain well. Heat the olive oil in the pan used to cook the spaghetti. Add the garlic and some freshly ground black pepper. Return the spaghetti to the pan, and add the sauce. Toss well. Serve immediately, topped with the pecorino cheese.

FARFALLE WITH BEEF, MUSHROOM AND SOUR CREAM

This is a luxurious dish using a prime cut of steak but, mixed with the pasta, a little beef goes a long way.

Serves 2-3

INGREDIENTS
8 ounces fillet or sirloin steak, sliced
2 tablespoons unsalted butter
1 onion, sliced
1¼ cups sliced mushrooms
1 tablespoon all-purpose flour
4 tablespoons sour cream
10 green olives, pitted and chopped
Salt and freshly ground black pepper
10 ounces farfalle (pasta bows)

Garnish
Sour cream
1 tablespoon freshly chopped parsley

Cut the meat into small, thin slices with a sharp knife. Melt half the butter, and fry the meat over a high heat until well browned. Remove the meat with a draining spoon, and set aside. Melt the remaining butter in the pan, and fry the onion slowly until soft and just beginning to color. Add the mushrooms, and cook for 3 minutes; then stir in the flour, and continue frying for an additional 3 minutes. Gradually stir in the sour cream, then add the meat, olives, and salt and pepper to taste.

Meanwhile, cook the farfalle in plenty of boiling, salted water for 10 minutes, or until tender but still firm. Drain well. Serve the pasta with the beef and mushroom sauce on top. Garnish with a little extra sour cream and chopped parsley.

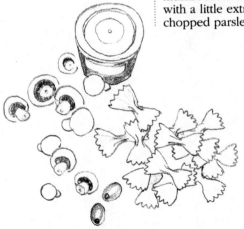

ITALIAN CASSEROLE

*Macaroni is used to thicken a savory sauce in this recipe,
turning it into a filling, family casserole.*

Serves 4

INGREDIENTS
3 ounces small macaroni
¼ cup butter or margarine
1 onion, chopped
1 clove garlic, crushed
2 14-ounce cans plum tomatoes
1 tablespoon tomato paste
1 red bell pepper, roughly
   chopped
1 green bell pepper, roughly
   chopped
8 ounces salami, cut into chunks
10 black olives, halved, and
   pitted
Salt and freshly ground black
   pepper
4 ounces mozzarella cheese,
   thinly sliced

Preheat the oven to 350°F. Cook the macaroni in plenty of boiling, salted water for 10 minutes, or until tender but still firm. Rinse under hot water, and drain well; then put into a shallow, ovenproof dish.

Meanwhile, melt the butter or margarine in a pan, and fry the onion and garlic slowly until soft. Add the undrained tomatoes, tomato paste, red and green bell peppers, salami and olives, and stir well. Simmer, uncovered, for 5 minutes, then season with salt and pepper to taste. Pour the sauce over the macaroni, stir, and cover with the sliced cheese. Bake, uncovered, for 20 minutes, until the cheese has melted. Serve immediately.

TAGLIATELLE WITH CREAMY LIVER SAUCE

I love chicken livers, especially in a creamy sauce with pasta.

Serves 4

INGREDIENTS

2 onions, sliced
1 clove garlic, crushed
4 tablespoons olive oil
1¼ cups sliced mushrooms
1 pound chicken livers, cleaned
   and sliced
½ cup light cream
2 eggs, beaten
Salt and freshly ground black
   pepper
10 ounces tagliatelle
Olive oil
1 tablespoon freshly chopped
   parsley

In a large skillet, cook the onions and garlic slowly in the oil until softened. Add the mushrooms, and cook for 3 minutes. Add the chicken livers to the onions and mushrooms, and cook until lightly browned. Remove the pan from the heat, and stir in the cream. Return to a low heat, and cook, uncovered, for 2 minutes longer. Remove from the heat, and stir in the lightly beaten eggs. Season with salt and pepper to taste.

Meanwhile, cook the tagliatelle in plenty of boiling salted water for 10 minutes, or until tender but still firm, stirring occasionally. Drain the tagliatelle, toss in a little olive oil and black pepper. Serve the sauce over the tagliatelle, and sprinkle with the parsley.

PASTITSIO

*This is a hearty bake, very similar to a traditional Maltese
dish which is actually topped with a pastry crust.*

Serves 4

INGREDIENTS

8 ounces macaroni
⅓ cup butter or margarine
½ cup grated Parmesan cheese
Pinch of grated nutmeg
Salt and freshly ground black
    pepper
2 eggs, beaten
1 onion, chopped
1 clove garlic, crushed
4 cups ground beef
2 tablespoons tomato paste
6 tablespoons beef stock
2 tablespoons freshly chopped
    parsley
4 tablespoons red wine
¼ cup all-purpose flour
1¼ cups milk

Preheat the oven to 375°F. Cook
the macaroni in plenty of boiling,
salted water for 10 minutes, or
until tender but still firm. Rinse
under hot water, and drain. Put
one-third of the butter or
margarine in the pan, and return
the macaroni to it. Add half the
cheese, the nutmeg, and salt and
pepper to taste. Let cool slightly;
then mix in half the beaten egg,
and set aside.

Melt half of the remaining butter
or margarine in a pan, and fry
the onion and garlic slowly until
the onion is soft. Increase the
heat; add the meat, and fry until
browned. Add the tomato paste,
stock, parsley and wine, and
season with salt and pepper.
Simmer for 20 minutes.

In a small pan, melt the rest of
the butter or margarine, then stir
in the flour and cook for 30
seconds. Remove from the heat,
and stir in the milk. Bring to a
boil, stirring continuously, until
the sauce thickens. Beat in the
remaining egg, and season to
taste. Spoon half the macaroni
into a serving dish, and cover
with the meat sauce. Add
another layer of macaroni. Pour
the white sauce over the
macaroni, and sprinkle with the
remaining cheese. Bake for 30
minutes until golden-brown.
Serve immediately.

226

MACARONI CHEESE WITH FRANKFURTERS

Macaroni cheese is one of my favorite lunch dishes – with frankfurters, it is very filling. Brown the dish under a hot broiler before serving, if preferred.

Serves 4

INGREDIENTS
8 frankfurters
1 pound macaroni
¼ cup butter or margarine
½ cup all-purpose flour
2½ cups milk
1½ cups grated Cheddar cheese
1 teaspoon mustard powder
Salt and freshly ground black
    pepper

Poach the frankfurters for 5-6 minutes in slightly salted boiling water. Skin the frankfurters if preferred, and slice the sausages diagonally.

Cook the macaroni in plenty of boiling, salted water for about 20 minutes, or until tender. Rinse in cold water, and drain well. Melt the butter or margarine in a saucepan. Stir in the flour, and cook for 1 minute. Remove the pan from the heat, and add the milk gradually, beating thoroughly. Return the pan to the heat. Bring to a boil, stirring continuously, then simmer for 2 minutes. Stir in the macaroni, frankfurters, grated cheese and mustard. Season to taste, and serve.

PORK & SHRIMP CHOW MEIN

Chow Mein is a noodle dish, flavored with small amounts of meat or fish and vegetables.

Serves 4-6

INGREDIENTS
- 8 ounces medium dried Chinese noodles
- 2 tablespoons oil
- 8 ounces pork tenderloin, thinly sliced
- 1 carrot, shredded
- 1 small red bell pepper, thinly sliced
- 1½ cups bean sprouts
- 2 ounces snow peas
- 1 tablespoon rice wine or dry sherry
- 2 tablespoons soy sauce
- ¾ cup shelled, cooked shrimp

Cook the noodles in plenty of boiling salted water for about 4-5 minutes. Rinse under hot water, and drain thoroughly.

Heat a wok or heavy-bottomed skillet, and add the oil. Stir-fry the pork for 4-5 minutes, or until almost cooked. Add the carrots to the pan, and cook for 1-2 minutes. Add the remaining vegetables, wine and soy sauce. Cook for about 2 minutes. Add the drained noodles and shrimp, and toss over the heat for 1-2 minutes. Serve immediately.

228

SPAGHETTI BOLOGNESE

This must surely be one of the most famous dishes in the world – it is certainly one of the most copied and abused! I hope you like this version.

Serves 4

INGREDIENTS
2 tablespoons butter or
  margarine
1 tablespoon olive oil
2 onions, finely chopped
1 carrot, diced
2 cups ground beef
½ cup canned tomato purée
Salt and freshly ground black
  pepper
1¼ cups brown beef stock
2 tablespoons sherry
10 ounces spaghetti
Grated Parmesan cheese

Heat the butter or margarine and oil in a pan, and cook the onions and carrot slowly until soft. Increase the heat, and add the ground beef. Fry for a few minutes; then stir, and continue cooking until the meat is browned all over. Add the tomato purée, salt and pepper and the stock. Simmer slowly for about 45 minutes, stirring occasionally, until the mixture thickens. Add the sherry to the sauce, and cook for 5 minutes longer. Meanwhile, bring a large pan of salted water to a boil; add the spaghetti, and cook for 10 minutes, or until *al dente*. Drain. Serve the spaghetti with the Bolognese sauce and grated Parmesan cheese.

FRIED NOODLES WITH PORK AND SHRIMP

Sambal ulek is a spicy Thai relish, used much as we would use chutney. When added to dishes during cooking, it gives a rich, hot flavor.

Serves 4

INGREDIENTS
8 ounces Chinese noodles
4 tablespoons oil
1 onion, finely chopped
2 cloves garlic, crushed
1 green chili, seeded and sliced
1 teaspoon sambal ulek
4 ounces pork, finely sliced
2 celery stalks, shredded
¼ head of bok-choi, shredded
1 tablespoon light soy sauce
4 ounces shelled and deveined
   shrimp
Salt and freshly ground black
   pepper

Garnish
Sliced cucumber
Sliced scallions

Soak the noodles in hot water for 8 minutes, or boil until cooked. Rinse in hot water, then let them drain in a colander.

Heat a wok or large skillet, and add the oil. Stir-fry the onion, garlic and chili until the onion begins to color. Add the sambal ulek, pork, celery, bok-choi and a pinch of salt and pepper. Stir-fry for 3 minutes. Add the soy sauce, drained noodles and shrimp, and toss the mixture to heat through well. Put into a warmed serving dish. Surround with sliced cucumber, and sprinkle the scallions on top.

SPICY STEAMED PORK WITH NOODLES

The combination of spicy meatballs, bok choy or spinach, noodles and fresh cilantro makes a simple but memorable dish.

Serves 4

INGREDIENTS
2 cups ground pork
1 teaspoon ground coriander
1 teaspoon ground cumin
1 teaspoon ground turmeric
1 bunch bok-choi or spinach, washed
1-2 tablespoons red or green curry paste
1 teaspoon shrimp paste
⅔ cup thick coconut milk
6 ounces egg noodles
Freshly chopped cilantro, to garnish

Put the pork and ground spices into a food processor, and process until very finely chopped. Shape the pork mixture into small balls, using dampened hands. Tear the bok choy into large pieces, and put into a heatproof dish that will fit into a steamer. Arrange the meat balls on top. Mix together the curry paste, shrimp paste and coconut milk, and pour over the meat balls. Cover and steam for 20 minutes. Meanwhile, cook the noodles as directed on the package. Drain well, then mix the noodles together with the pork and bok-choi or spinach. Garnish with a sprinkling of chopped cilantro leaves.

CANNELLONI

Cannelloni should be cooked in a very hot oven to crisp the top of the pasta, while leaving most of the dish tender and moist.

Serves 4

INGREDIENTS
Filling
1 tablespoon olive oil
2 cloves garlic, crushed
1 onion, chopped
4 cups ground beef
1 teaspoon tomato paste
1 tablespoon freshly chopped basil
1 tablespoon freshly chopped oregano
8 ounces frozen spinach, thawed
1 egg, lightly beaten
4 tablespoons heavy cream
Salt and freshly ground black pepper

12 cannelloni tubes
2 tablespoons grated Parmesan cheese

Tomato sauce
1 tablespoon olive oil
1 onion, chopped
1 clove garlic, crushed
14-ounce can chopped tomatoes
2 tablespoons tomato paste
Salt and freshly ground black pepper

Béchamel sauce
1¼ cups milk
1 slice of onion
3 peppercorns
1 small bay leaf
2 tablespoons butter or margarine
¼ cup all-purpose flour
Salt and freshly ground black pepper

Prepare the filling. Heat the oil in a pan, and fry the garlic and onion slowly until soft and transparent. Add the beef, and cook, stirring continuously, until well browned. Drain off any fat. Add the tomato paste, basil and oregano, and cook slowly for 15 minutes. Add the spinach, egg and cream, and salt and pepper to taste.

Cook the cannelloni in a large pan of boiling, salted water for 15-20 minutes, until tender. Rinse in hot water, and drain. Carefully fill the tubes with the meat mixture, using a piping bag with a wide, plain tip, or a teaspoon.

Preheat the oven to 450°F. Make the tomato sauce. Heat the oil in a pan. Add the onion and garlic, and cook slowly until transparent. Press the tomatoes through a strainer, and add to the pan with the tomato paste, salt and pepper. Bring to a boil, and then simmer for 5 minutes. Set aside.

To make the béchamel sauce, put the milk into a pan with the onion, peppercorns and bay leaf. Heat slowly for 1 minute, taking care not to boil, and set aside to cool for 5 minutes. Strain. Melt the butter or margarine in a pan. Remove it from the heat, and stir in the flour; then gradually add the milk. Bring to a boil, stirring continuously, until the sauce boils and thickens. Season to taste.

Spread the tomato sauce in the bottom of an ovenproof dish. Lay the cannelloni on top, and cover with the béchamel sauce. Sprinkle with the grated cheese, and bake for 10-15 minutes. Serve immediately.

MEAT RAVIOLI

Ravioli are little packages of pasta, traditionally with a meat filling. Homemade ravioli bears little resemblance to the rather nondescript ravioli sold in cans – do try this recipe.

Serves 4

INGREDIENTS
Filling
¼ cup butter or margarine
1 clove garlic, crushed
1 onion, grated
2 cups ground beef
5 tablespoons red wine
Salt and freshly ground black
   pepper
2 tablespoons breadcrumbs
¾ cup chopped cooked spinach
2 eggs, beaten

Dough
2¼ cups white bread flour   .
3 eggs, lightly beaten

Sauce
14-ounce can chopped tomatoes
1 small onion, grated
1 small carrot, finely diced
1 bay leaf
2 parsley stalks
Salt and freshly ground black
   pepper
½ cup grated Parmesan cheese

Prepare the filling. Melt the butter or margarine in a pan. Add the garlic and onion, and fry slowly for 1 minute. Add the ground beef, and fry until browned. Add the red wine, salt and pepper, and cook, uncovered, for 15 minutes. Strain the juices, and reserve them for the sauce. Let the filling cool, then add the bread crumbs, chopped spinach, and beaten eggs to bind. Add salt and pepper to taste.

To make the dough, sift the flour into a bowl. Make a well in the center, and add the eggs. Work the flour and eggs together with a fork, then knead by hand, until a smooth dough is formed. Wrap the dough in plastic wrap, and let rest for 15 minutes in a cool place. Lightly flour a board, and roll the dough out thinly into a rectangle. Cut the dough in half.

Put small piles of the filling about 1½ inches apart on one half of the dough. Put the remaining dough on top, and cut with a ravioli cutter or small cooky cutter. Seal the edges by pinching together.

Cook the ravioli in batches in a large, wide pan with plenty of boiling, salted water until tender – about 8 minutes. Remove the ravioli carefully with a draining spoon.

To make the sauce, put all the ingredients into a saucepan. Add the reserved juice from the cooked meat, and bring to a boil. Simmer for 10 minutes. Press the sauce through a strainer, and return the smooth sauce to the pan. Adjust the seasoning. Put the ravioli in a warmed serving dish, and cover with the tomato sauce. Serve immediately with grated Parmesan cheese.

LASAGNE

Lasagne, a glorious dish of layered pasta, meat sauce and fragrant white sauce, is best made with fresh pasta. If using dried, choose a lasagne which requires precooking – it only takes a few minutes, and the flavor is so much better than the no-cook variety.

Serves 4

INGREDIENTS
8 sheets lasagne

Meat sauce
¼ cup butter or margarine
1 onion, chopped
1 celery stalk, sliced
2 carrots, diced
1 cup ground beef
1 tablespoon all-purpose flour
1 tablespoon tomato paste
⅔ cup beef stock
1 teaspoon freshly chopped marjoram
Salt and freshly ground black pepper

Béchamel sauce
1¼ cups milk
6 black peppercorns
Slice of onion
1 bay leaf
Parsley stalks
¼ cup butter or margarine
⅓ cup all-pupose flour

Prepare the meat sauce. Melt the butter or margarine in a pan. Add the onion, celery and carrot, and cook until the onion is golden. Add the ground beef, and brown well; then stir in the flour, and add the tomato paste, beef stock, marjoram, and salt and pepper. Simmer for 15 minutes.

Meanwhile, cook the lasagne in plenty of boiling salted water for 10 minutes, or until tender. Rinse in cold water, and drain carefully. Lay the lasagne out on a clean cloth to dry.

Prepare the béchamel sauce. Bring the milk almost to a boil in a saucepan with the peppercorns, onion, bay leaf and parsley stalks, then remove from the heat. Let cool for 5 minutes, then pour through a strainer to remove the flavorings. Melt the butter or margarine in a saucepan; then stir in the flour, and cook for 30 seconds. Remove the pan from the heat, and gradually add the milk, stirring continuously. Bring to a boil, then simmer for 3 minutes.

Grease an ovenproof baking dish. Line the bottom with a layer of lasagne. Cover with a layer of meat sauce, then a layer of béchamel sauce. Add another layer of lasagne, repeating the layers until all the ingredients are used, finishing with a layer of béchamel sauce. Bake for about 20 minutes, or until the top is golden. Serve immediately.

SWEET PASTA DESSERTS

Not all pasta dishes have to be savory! There are many sweet dishes, usually made with macaroni or one of the other, smaller pasta shapes, that are delicious, especially to serve after a light main course to satisfy a hearty appetite. Pasta puddings are also useful dishes for those who have lost their appetite and are unwell, as a few spoonfuls of a milky pudding will introduce both protein and carbohydrate, as well as a little fat, to the invalid's diet.

Pasta and Fruit

Just as pasta and vegetables provide so many winning combinations of flavors for savory dishes, so pasta and fruits provide a versatile selection of basic dishes for desserts. I shall not pretend that they are ever likely to be the most sophisticated of dishes, but they are good, honest fare suitable for family meals and informal entertaining.

Many fruits go well with pasta, and their seasonal availability suggests whether the dish should be hot or cold. For example, summer fruits, such as peaches and strawberries, make surprise bases for brulées, the fruit hidden away in the bottom of a dish under a thick layer of creamy pasta, then topped with caramelized sugar and served chilled. I like to cook apricots, plums and damsons to a thick purée, and then serve that swirled into a dish of sweet pasta. A recipe for Creamy Macaroni with Apricot Purée is included in this chapter.

Successful Sweet Pasta Desserts

Desserts are best made with small or thin pastas. When I was a child, my mother used to buy thin macaroni for desserts, but this is not so widely available now, so the short-cut, quick-cook macaroni may be used, or vermicelli. Small pastini, the pasta shapes for soup, are also excellent for dessert dishes.

I find that a sweet pasta mix is far more likely to boil over during cooking than a rice dessert, so I cook the pasta in a large pan on the stove top where I can keep an eye on it. Choose a pan that will provide plenty of room for the pasta to cook without sticking together, and will let the milk simmer without boiling over. When the pasta is tender, the mixture may be transferred to an ovenproof dish, and baked to produce a crisp top, as for a traditional rice dessert.

Vermicelli is really best cooked in boiling water, before being added to other ingredients after cooking, as in the recipe for Honey Vermicelli. If the vermicelli is not boiled quickly enough, the strands will stick together in a solid mass, and it is difficult to keep a pan of milk boiling sufficiently quickly to prevent that from happening, without the milk boiling over.

A Pasta Dessert for a Sophisticated Meal

I have said before that pasta desserts are good, honest, family fare. Well, I have included one recipe here which is an exception to the rule, a sweet ravioli in a sour cream sauce. If you are an experienced ravioli-maker, you will think nothing of producing this sweet version of a favorite stuffed pasta. However, inexperienced ravioli-makers should not be daunted, or discouraged from making this dish. It is actually a very good recipe for entertaining because the ravioli may be made ahead, so may the cherry sauce and cream mixture, and then the sauce may just be reheated while the ravioli is cooking.

The cherry ravioli is best made with fresh, tart black cherries, but as these are not always easy to obtain, the recipe specifies canned cherries. Do make certain that the cherries are very well drained before they are put into the ravioli. If they are too moist, they will not only make the pasta sticky, but will make it difficult to handle, clinging to the work surface during shaping. If the ravioli are not to be cooked immediately, I would transfer them to a lightly floured, clean dishcloth to dry – do not leave them on the work surface where they have been made, or they will stick.

The Ninth Jewel in Eight-Treasure Dessert

The Chinese are not big dessert eaters except at banquets, when their most famous rice dessert, Eight-Jewel or Eight-Treasure Dessert is served. This is served either as a molded dessert, filled with a variety of fruits, or as a creamy rice dessert with the fruits mixed into it. I have adapted a recipe for the latter to be made with thin macaroni.

BLACK CHERRY RAVIOLI
WITH SOUR CREAM SAUCE

Ravioli may be savory or sweet – these are filled with tart black cherries.

Serves 4

INGREDIENTS
Dough
2¼ cups white bread flour
1 tablespoon sugar
3 eggs, lightly beaten

1 pound can black cherries, pitted
1 teaspoon arrowroot
¼ cup granulated sugar
½ cup sour cream
½ cup heavy cream

Empty the cherries into a strainer. Drain off and reserve the juice.

Make the dough by sifting the flour and sugar into a bowl. Make a well in the center, and add the lightly beaten eggs. Work the flour and eggs together with a spoon, and then by hand, until a smooth dough is formed. Knead gently until smooth and shiny. Lightly flour a board, and roll the dough out thinly into a rectangle. Cut the dough in half. Put the well-drained cherries about 1½ inches apart on the dough. Put the remaining dough on top, and cut with a small glass or cooky cutter. Seal well around the edges with the back of a fork.

Boil plenty of water in a large saucepan, then drop in the cherry pasta. Cook for about 10 minutes, or until they rise to the surface. Remove with a draining spoon, and keep warm. Reserve 2 tablespoons of the cherry juice. Mix 1 tablespoon with the arrowroot. Mix any remaining juice with the sugar, and put over a medium heat. Add the arrowroot mixture, and heat until it boils and thickens. Meanwhile, mix the sour cream and heavy cream together, and marble the remaining 1 tablespoon of cherry juice through it. Pour the hot, thickened cherry juice over the cherry ravioli. Serve hot, with the cream sauce.

HONEY VERMICELLI

Honey, sesame and cinnamon give a Greek flavor to this pasta dessert.

Serves 4

INGREDIENTS
8 ounces vermicelli
¼ cup butter
2 teaspoons sesame seeds
3 tablespoons clear honey
¼ teaspoon cinnamon

Sauce
5 tablespoons heavy cream
5 tablespoons sour cream

Cook the vermicelli in boiling water for 5 minutes, or until tender, stirring regularly with a fork to separate the noodles. Drain, and spread out to dry on a wire tray covered with paper towels or a dishcloth. Leave for about an hour.

Make the sauce by mixing the sour cream and heavy cream together. Melt the butter in a skillet. Add the sesame seeds, and fry until lightly browned. Stir in the honey, cinnamon and vermicelli, and heat slowly. Serve hot, topped with the cream sauce.

CHOCOLATE CREAM
HÉLÈNE

*Pears and chocolate are a classic combination – with a
pasta cream the dessert is a little more substantial.*

Serves 4

INGREDIENTS
3 ounces small pasta shapes for
  soup
2 cups milk
3 tablespoons superfine sugar
1 teaspoon cocoa powder
1 tablespoon hot water
⅔ cup heavy or whipping cream,
  lightly whipped
15-ounce can pear halves

Decoration
Grated chocolate

Cook the pasta in the milk and
sugar until soft. Stir frequently,
being careful not to let the milk
boil over. Meanwhile, dissolve
the cocoa powder in hot water,
then stir it into the pasta. Pour
the pasta into a bowl to cool.
When cool, fold in the lightly
whipped cream, then chill. Serve
the pasta cream with the pear
halves, and a sprinkling of grated
chocolate.

CREAM CHEESE
MARGHERITA

I usually think of a margherita as a drink or a pizza! Here it's a delicious pasta dessert.

Serves 4

INGREDIENTS
⅓ cup golden raisins
Grated peel and juice of ½ lemon
4 ounces small pasta shapes for soup
1 cup cream cheese
¼ cup superfine sugar
⅔ cup light cream
½ teaspoon ground cinnamon

Decoration
1 tablespoon slivered almonds
Lemon peel, cut into slivers

Soak the golden raisins in the lemon juice for about 1 hour. Meanwhile, cook the pasta in plenty of boiling water until tender, stirring occasionally. Drain and cool. Beat the cream cheese, sugar and cream together until smooth, then beat in the grated lemon rind and cinnamon. Fold in the pasta and golden raisins. Divide between individual dessert glasses or dishes, then cover the tops with slivered almonds and slivers of lemon peel. Chill before serving.

VANILLA CREAM MELBA

*Sweet pasta desserts make substantial desserts to serve after a
light main course of salad.*

Serves 4

INGREDIENTS
3 ounces small pasta shapes for
    soup
2 cups milk
¼ cup brown sugar
Few drops of vanilla extract
⅔ cup heavy or whipping cream,
    lightly whipped
15-ounce can peach halves
1 teaspoon cinnamon (optional)

Melba sauce
1½ cups raspberries
About 3 tablespoons
    confectioners' sugar

Cook the pasta in the milk and
sugar until soft. Stir frequently,
being careful not to let the milk
boil over. Take off the heat, and
stir in the vanilla extract. Pour
the pasta into a bowl to cool.
When cool, fold in the cream,
and chill.

Meanwhile, make the Melba
sauce. Press the raspberries
through a strainer, then mix in
confectioners' sugar to the
desired thickness and taste. Serve
the pasta with the peach halves
and Melba sauce. Dust with
cinnamon if liked.

244

SPAGHETTI DOLCE

This is a very simple pasta, a nursery dessert for big children!
I leave the spaghetti in long strands – the sauce is so delicious
to suck up with the pasta.

Serves 4

INGREDIENTS
6 ounces spaghetti
⅔ cup heavy cream
2 tablespoons brandy
Superfine sugar to taste

Cook the spaghetti in plenty of boiling water until just tender but still firm. Drain and rinse in boiling water; then drain again, and put the spaghetti into a warm serving dish. Mix together the cream, brandy and sugar, and pour over the hot spaghetti. Toss, then serve immediately.

EIGHT-TREASURE MACARONI

This is a variation on the classic Chinese dessert of Eight-Treasure Rice. I find the dessert slightly less rich when made with macaroni.

Serves 4

INGREDIENTS
6 ounces macaroni
1¼ cups heavy cream
1 cup sweetened chestnut purée
15 dried red dates
2 tablespoons large raisins
½ cup walnut halves
¼ cup almonds
⅓ cup halved candied cherries
2 tablespoons chopped angelica
⅓ cup chopped candied papaya
   or mango

Cook the macaroni in plenty of boiling water until just tender but still firm. Drain, and rinse in boiling water; then drain again. Return the macaroni to the saucepan, and stir in the cream and chestnut purée. Heat slowly until the chestnut purée has melted into the macaroni.

Roughly chop the dates, raisins and nuts, and add them to the warm macaroni with the remaining ingredients. Stir carefully, then serve the dessert warm.

PEACH BRULÉE

*The combination of peaches and creamy macaroni make
this a real brulée surprise.*

Serves 4

INGREDIENTS
4 ounces small pasta shapes for
  soup
2 large, ripe peaches
Scant 1 cup heavy cream, lightly
  whipped
¼ cup superfine sugar
Brown crystal (demerara) sugar

Cook the pasta in plenty of
boiling salted water for about 5
minutes, until just tender but still
firm. Drain, and rinse in cold
water; then drain again. Cut the
peaches in half, and remove the
skin and pits. Fan each half into
the bottom of a large ramekin or
small ovenproof dish.

Mix the cooled pasta with the
whipped cream, then stir in the
superfine sugar to taste. Spoon
the mixture into the ramekins,
over the peaches. Leave until
quite cold.

Preheat the broiler until very hot.
Put a thick layer of brown crystal
sugar all over the top of the
creamed macaroni, then quickly
broil the sugar until it has melted
and caramelized. Chill the
brulées lightly before serving.

HONEY & CARDAMOM MACARONI

Honey and cardamom make the most delightful aromatic flavorings for this macaroni dessert.

Serves 4

INGREDIENTS
4 ounces macaroni
2 cups full-cream milk
3-4 tablespoons clear honey, to taste
1 teaspoon cardamom seeds, lightly ground
⅔ cup crème fraîche
Grated lemon peel, to decorate

Put the macaroni, milk and honey into a large pan, and cook until the macaroni is soft. Stir frequently, being careful not to let the milk boil over. Take the pan off the heat, and stir in the ground cardamom seeds. Let the macaroni cool slightly, then stir in the crème fraîche. Pour into a serving dish, and top with grated lemon peel before serving.

CREAMY MACARONI WITH APRICOT PURÉE

A slightly sharp apricot purée makes an excellent sauce to serve with a dish of rich, sweet pasta.

Serves 4

INGREDIENTS
1 pound fresh apricots, or 1½ cups no-soak dried apricots
⅔ cup water
Grated peel and juice of 1 lemon
½ cup superfine sugar
6 ounces macaroni
1¼ cups heavy cream

Prepare the apricot purée. Pit the apricots if using fresh, and put them into a pan with the water, lemon peel and juice.

Cover and simmer for about 10 minutes, or until soft. Press the fruit through a strainer, or purée in a blender or food processor until smooth. Add ¼ cup-⅓ cup of the superfine sugar, or to taste, and a little extra water if necessary.

While the apricots are cooking, bring a large pan of water to a boil. Add the macaroni, and cook until just tender but still firm. Drain and rinse in boiling water, then drain again. Heat the cream slowly with the remaining sugar; then add the cooked macaroni, and toss well. Serve the pasta with the apricot purée marbled through it.

INDEX